I. F. STONE

A Portrait

I. F. STONE

A Portrait

ANDREW PATNER

ANCHOR BOOKS
DOUBLEDAY
NEW YORK   LONDON   TORONTO   SYDNEY   AUCKLAND

An Anchor Book

PUBLISHED BY DOUBLEDAY

a division of Bantam Doubleday Dell Publishing Group, Inc.
666 Fifth Avenue, New York, New York 10103

ANCHOR BOOKS, DOUBLEDAY, and the portrayal of an anchor
are trademarks of Doubleday, a division of Bantam Doubleday
Dell Publishing Group, Inc.

I.F. Stone: A Portrait was originally published
in hardcover by Pantheon Books in 1988.
The Anchor Books edition is published by arrangement
with Pantheon Books.

Grateful acknowledgment is made to Penguin Books Ltd.
for permission to reprint "None Is More Wonderful than Man" Chorus
by Sophocles from *The Penguin Book of Greek Verse*,
Penguin Books, 1971, pp. 203-4.
Copyright © 1971 by Constantine A. Trypanis.

Library of Congress Cataloging-in-Publication Data
Patner, Andrew.
  I. F. Stone: a portrait / Andrew Patner.
  —1st Anchor Books ed.
    p.   cm.
  1. Stone, I. F. (Isidor F.), 1907–   —Biography.
2. Journalists—
—United States—Biography.   I. Title.
PN4874.S69P38   1990   89-71505
070′.92—dc20   CIP
[B]
ISBN 0-385-41382-3

To give a little comfort to the oppressed, to write the truth exactly as I saw it, to make no compromises other than those of quality imposed by my own inadequacies, to be free to follow no master other than my own compulsions, to live up to my idealized image of what a true newspaperman should be, and still be able to make a living for my family—what more could a man ask?

Philosophically I believe that a man's life reduces itself ultimately to a faith—the fundamental is beyond proof—and that faith is a matter of aesthetics, a sense of beauty and harmony. I think every man is his own Pygmalion, and spends his life fashioning himself. And in fashioning himself, for good or ill, he fashions the human race and its future.

> I. F. Stone
> "Notes on Closing, But Not in Farewell"
> *I. F. Stone's Weekly*, December 14, 1971

The one thing in the world, of value, is the active soul.

> Ralph Waldo Emerson
> "The American Scholar," 1837

To the memory of
my grandparents,
who gave me everything
of value in my life,

To the one
who picked up
more of what I dropped
than anyone ever has
before,
              and

To I. F. Stone,
his own Pygmalion,
who fashioned himself
for good
and thus helped to fashion
the human race
and its future
(and who found the quote
from Tibullus)

CONTENTS

CONTENTS

ACKNOWLEDGMENTS

My thanks must go to a number of people. My parents stood by me through what was a difficult period for all of us. They are witty, warm, and wise. They can lick anybody else's parents any time. My friends Kenny Blum, Claudia J. Keenan, Kira E. Foster, W. Vance Baker, M.D., and Ron Burg helped in more ways than they may be aware of. Michael Bless, James Alan McPherson, and Dr. Harold Balikov all provided important support at crucial times. Lindsay Roberts and Richard Warren Shepro know the work—as well as the rewards—of friendship, as does Sunny Haskin, M.D. Of Professor Paul Boyer, now Merle Curti Professor of History at the University of Wisconsin at Madison, I will simply say that he is a *mensch*. His patience, kindness, and understanding are apparently boundless. That this work is not what it might have been is only because I did not seek or heed his counsel more often.

Esther M. (Mrs. I. F.) Stone and Studs Terkel were instrumental in arranging my interviews with I. F. Stone. My cousin, Leslie Levy Mirchin, was a gracious host and also helped me to understand Stone's changing relationship with the State of Israel, a subject that I will have to continue to pursue at another time. Professor Thomas McCormick, of the University of Wisconsin, Professor Stephen E. Ambrose, of the University of New Orleans, and Professor Fredrick Blum, of Chicago State University, generously shared insights with me on Stone's standing among establishment academics, both traditionalists and "revisionists."

George Anastaplo, of the Loyola University School of Law and the University of Chicago, listened to portions of a draft and later read an early version of the manuscript, on each occasion making useful suggestions. He and his wife, Sara Prince Anastaplo, patiently assisted me with sections of the text involving Ancient Greek. Karen Wierer's professionalism and skill in typing and retyping a difficult manuscript are exceeded only by her patience and good humor. Marianne McNicholas also provided important typing assistance, for which I am grateful.

An integral part of this project was an oral presentation that I made at the University of Wisconsin in early 1984, "I. F. Stone: The Last Radical American Journalist?" I am especially thankful to Eli Goldblatt, Michael Berkowitz, and Bruce Muck, in addition to others mentioned above, for their perceptive questions and criticism at that time.

Special acknowledgment is made of: Memorial Library at the University of Wisconsin at Madison; the British Library of the British Museum; the Joseph Regenstein Library of the University of Chicago; the Chicago Public Library; the Library of Congress; the Center for Research Libraries and the Murray-Green Library of Roosevelt University (both in Chicago), all of whose collections, facilities, and staff assistance I made use of; and the State Historical Society of Wisconsin, whose borrowing privileges I abused, though they made me pay in blood. I also wish to thank Robert Charles Cottrell for permission (through I. F. Stone) to examine his unpublished doctoral dissertation, "Wielding the Pen as a Sword: The Radical

ACKNOWLEDGMENTS

Journalist I. F. Stone," University of Oklahoma, 1983, and Jerry Bruck, Jr., who furnished me with a transcript of his 1973 film, *I. F. Stone's Weekly*.

Grateful thanks must go again to Studs Terkel and to David Halberstam, both of whom encouraged me to seek a publisher for the manuscript. As a first-time author I could not have been more fortunate than to find myself with Pantheon Books. I will always be indebted to André Schiffrin, who saw that there was a book here; to James Peck, for his sensitive and sensible treatment throughout; and to Jenna Laslocky and Ginny Read, for boundless patience, good advice, and kindness.

My debt to I. F. Stone himself is considerable; its scope is indicated in the dedication. My attempt to repay it is what follows.

Andrew Patner

Hyde Park, Chicago
June 1987

NOTE

Much of the following material is drawn from conversations I had with I. F. Stone on April 20, 21, 22, and 25, 1984. These talks took place in a variety of settings (or walkings) in Washington, D.C.: the Library of Congress, a five-mile route from the Capitol to Dupont Circle, two restaurants, a supermarket, a three-mile stretch of parkway, and Stone's home in Northwest Washington. We had further talks in Washington on March 21 and 22, 1987. Some portions of this book are drawn from a discussion I. F. Stone had with participants in the Department for International Journalism of the University of Southern California on March 21, 1987, at the International Center for Development Policy, in Washington. I wish to acknowledge Murray Fromson, director of the Department, for kindly permitting me to attend this session. I transcribed and edited the tapes of all these sessions myself and have edited out most of my questions, comments, and interruptions. Although I have edited also for style and sense, with rare exceptions I have not transposed or interpolated sections of our discussions. They appear here substantially as they occurred. Ellipses indicate pauses, not omissions of words. I have interspersed extended excerpts from these transcripts with sections offering historical background as well as my own observations and analysis.

Many wonders there are, and yet none is more wonderful than man. He journeys over the grey ocean with stormy Notos (the south wind) crossing through waves that surge about him; Earth, the immortal, the greatest of the gods, the tireless one, he wears away, turning the soil with his horses as his ploughs pass up and down, year after year.

With woven nets he snares the race of thoughtless birds, the tribes of savage beasts, the sea-brood of the deep, man of subtle wit. By his cunning he masters the animals that nest in the wilderness, that roam across the hills; he tames the rich-maned horse, putting a yoke upon its neck, and the unwearied mountain bull.

And he has taught himself speech and wind-swift thought, and the ways of building an ordered state, and he has taught himself to escape the arrows of the frost and of the rain, when it is hard to sleep under the open sky—the all-resourceful; he is never at a loss whatever comes his way. Only from death will he not devise an escape; although he has found ways of curing hopeless sicknesses.

How skilful, passing belief, are the arts that lead him sometimes to evil and sometimes to good! When he honours the laws of the land and justice sanctioned by the gods, his cities stand proud and tall; but he who rashly embraces evil is homeless. May the man who acts thus never share my hearth, or my thoughts.

Sophocles
"Chorus on Man," *Antigone*
tr. C. A. Trypanis

I. F. STONE

A Portrait

1

LIBRARY OF CONGRESS

"Now we're looking for Libanius. I think they have a French translation of his *Autobiography*. Maybe it's German. I think it's French. You might have noticed that that one *Apology* in the card catalogue was the *Apology of Socrates* of Libanius, not by Plato or Xenophon. Very few people know about the Libanius. Fourth century A.D. He was a close associate of the Emperor Julian. You know who Julian was?"

"He gave us Christianity?"

"No, he tried to get rid of it. He tried to revive paganism. That's why he was known as Julian the Apostate."

"I did have this in Western Civilization, but it's all emptying out."

"The trouble with getting all of Western Civilization over a semester is that it's like a jet flight across the United States: 'Hey, there's the Mississippi River! There's the Grand Canyon! Hey, that's the Pacific Ocean! By goll! I've seen the whole United States!' "

We are in the rotunda of the Library of Congress in Washington, D.C., on a Friday morning, April 20, 1984. Two of us. The one who knows Julian from Constantine is Isidor Feinstein Stone, I. F. Stone, or, to many, "Izzy" Stone. Born on December 24, 1907, in Philadelphia, Stone has been a journalist for over sixty years. He has also been,

3

for roughly the same amount of time, a devoted amateur of the ancients. Especially the ancient Greeks. And right now, especially Libanius. Fourth century A.D. The other fellow—the one with the jet-flight introduction to Western Civilization—is myself. Born on December 17, 1959, in Chicago. So the calendar gives Stone a good fifty-two years on me. But that isn't half of the story. Because Stone has been working all of that time with an energy that I have never even approached. Even on my better days. And right now, it is all I can do to keep up with him. Even with a tape recorder *and* a note pad.

It wasn't quite what I was expecting. Stone had tried to put me off of an interview. His health was not good, he had told me over the phone (that is, when he *would* talk to me on the phone). And he'd been interviewed a thousand times, so what more was there for him to say? And besides, he was devoting what time he had to the Greeks. He was trying to show how he could have got Socrates off if he'd been his lawyer. You see, it was a civil liberties case and, well, he didn't want to get into it over the phone—his hearing wasn't so good. And he had to finish a piece for the *Nation* on President Reagan's "Star Wars" defense proposals. You see, he'd read through some documents and found that even Richard Perle ("and this guy is a terrible hawk") had serious reservations about the effectiveness of a space shield. So the point was, he was sorry, but he just didn't have the time.

Though this was all happening at a time when I very much wanted to take no for an answer, something in me spoke up for perseverance. So I tried some mutual friends and acquaintances. Most of these efforts didn't work out, but Studs Terkel came through, and, I'll be candid, *Mrs.* Stone was on my side. The call came to me in Madison, in mid-April. If I was going to be in Washington, he might have an hour or so, but that was it and it certainly wasn't worth making a special trip. He was entitled to his interpretation, but I was on my way to Washington.

Once there, Stone had second thoughts. He had to go down to the Library of Congress to find some books ("some pretty rare items"), but maybe I could meet him there. We could have a cup of tea, but that was all the time he had. What did I look like?—he had bad eyes, you know. Did I know what he looked like? Yes, I said (figuring that no one looks too unlike his caricature by David Levine). Did *I* have good eyes? Not as good as Hemingway's, but I thought I could spot him. Good, he'd meet me in an hour in the card catalogue. And that's how we got to looking for Libanius.

"Here we have *Selected Works.*"
"Is that the beginning?"
"Yes. This is from the Loeb Library."
"That I have."
"Now, there's *Discours moraux.* Moral discourses. And the same thing, but a British edition. I'm translating here: 'Friendship, the Insatisfaction,' 'The Richness of Unhappiness and Poverty,' 'Of Poverty and Friendship,' 'Of Slavery.' Are you interested in any of those?"
"Yeah. I think I am. I didn't know about that one. What's next?"
"Now we have a German *Autobiographical Works* of Libanius."

"Oh, 'works,' or 'work'?"

"Well, *Schriften*, is that . . ."

"It's 'works.' That's the *Autobiography*. So give me a call number on that."

"Now there's the same thing with the Greek text and English."

"Oh, I'd rather have that. Oh boy! How many pages is that?"

"Two hundred and forty-four."

"Oh, not bad."

"Now Greek. I'm testing my transliteration skills here: *Basilikos*?"

"Oh . . ." Stone takes a look. "*Basilika*. It's an encomium on the dead Caesar, Constantine. King or royal . . ."

"*Themistius in Libanius' Brieven*. I guess that's in German? Letters, selections of letters."

"That's Dutch, not German. Those are references to Themistius in his correspondence."

"Aelius Aristides . . ."

"Oh . . ." He reads: " 'Against . . . *Antinus*, *Libanius*, *declamatus*, *pro Socrate*, *Aristotiumus* . . .' Oh Jesus! Jesus! That's his answer to the *Apology of Socrates*. Oh gee . . . by Demetrius of Phalerum—he was long before Libanius. Oh boy, I better make a note of that. Aelius Aristides. I've got a lot of his works at home. But this is a very rare work, from the Library of St. Mark's in Venice.

"We've got everything now. Are you, as a growing boy, hungry? I don't have lunch, but I'll treat you."

And so, fifteen minutes turned into nine hours, spread out over five meetings that week in Washington. Stone talked with me about his current interests and his past ones. But I found them remarkably similar. From his early boyhood, Stone was interested in the idea of human freedom, particularly freedom of thought and of ideas. He was drawn equally to ancient Greece and to American radicalism, as he was to language and literature. And he showed from those early years an astonishing capacity for hard work and a strong respect for others who worked as hard and did as good a job. There are three simple nouns, names of occupations, that when pronounced by Stone are infused with all of his feelings about their special place in—or their relation to—society: *writer*, *scholar*, and *newspaperman*. Though he is given to descriptive adjectives as well (*beautiful* and *wonderful* are his favorites when it comes time to praise; less printable ones when he seeks to damn), these three nouns usually stand alone in his speech. They are, for Stone, true vocations rather than mere jobs. But they also evoke craft and skill. And independence.

It is hard to see Stone as a "team player." Though a lifelong advocate of socialism, he has worked best when he has worked alone. Though much of his independence may be the result of circumstances—the McCarthy-era blacklist, intermittent bouts of deafness—more of it seems the result of temperament. Disappointed with establishment education (he left college at the age of twenty, without a degree) and with establishment journalism, he found success as the proprietor of a one-man newspaper, and happiness as a self-made scholar, teaching himself Greek line by painful line and offering the results of his investigations into the ancient world to packed university auditoriums around the country. Of course the man who first

7

impelled his interest, Kropotkin, had a vision that was both anarchistic and romantic. And the man who both repels and fascinates him in his later years, Socrates, can be seen as the world's first and greatest professional loner.

This book is an attempt to get a handle on the multi-faceted Stone by looking at his careers as newspaperman, writer, and scholar. It will discuss also his writings and the attitudes he expressed in our talks, with the hope of understanding the forces that shaped him and his values. Along the way I hope to provide readers a glimpse of Stone's personality—the breadth of his learning and humanity, his senses of humor and outrage, and the depth of his optimism in a world that seems to others increasingly dark.

2

SKETCH

I had learned about Herbert Spencer and there
were very few places in town that had books.
And I got wind of the fact that there was a Mrs.
Groves whose father had been a free thinker and
died and left quite a few books, and I found out
that she had Herbert Spencer's *First Principles*. I
came home from school one day and my mother
said, "Mrs. Groves came around today, and we
had a very odd conversation. She wanted to know
if you were an invalid. So I said, 'No, Isadore's
not an invalid. He's not *sports*, but he's not an invalid.' And then she asked if she could loan you
some book you had asked her for. And I said,
'He's a great reader, he reads everything.' " Then
I realized that she had come around to ask my
mother if I was an *infidel*. This was a very church
town, and she wanted to clear things with my
mother before she gave me such a heretical book.

IN A JOURNALISTIC CAREER that has spanned more than six
decades, I. F. Stone has been called many things, but nothing
so off the mark as the suggestion by the lady in Haddonfield,
New Jersey, to Mrs. Feinstein that her son Isadore might be
an infidel. For Isadore Feinstein, who, in 1937, would become
I. F. Stone, is a believer, and has been one of the most faithful

practitioners of journalism in American history. From his first experiments as an editor-publisher while still in high school in the early 1920s, through work as an editorial writer for the Philadelphia *Record* and the New York *Post*, tenures as Washington editor for the *Nation*, stints as a columnist for *PM*, the New York *Star*, and the *Daily Compass*, to his nineteen years as owner-editor-author-proofreader of *I. F. Stone's Weekly*, and his years as a contributor and contributing editor for the *New York Review of Books*, Stone has tried to live up to the twin ideals of progressive social change and "the idealized image of what a true newspaperman should be."

I. F. Stone is the son of Russian-Jewish immigrants who were moderately successful as shopkeepers. (The spelling of his first name varies. His given name appears originally to have been spelled *Isadore*, but when he wrote under the name Feinstein, he spelled it *Isidor*.) A voracious reader from an early age, by high school Stone had consumed the works of Whitman, Keats, Shelley, Wordsworth, Spencer, Heraclitus, Cervantes, Gibbon, Emerson, Thoreau, Charles and Mary Beard, Stephen Crane, and Jack London. The classics intrigued him (in college he taught himself to read two books of Lucretius's *De rerum natura* in Latin and one poem of Sappho's in Greek); the moderns radicalized him. London's *Martin Eden*, essays by Engels, and Kropotkin's *The Conquest of Bread* convinced him that there were political alternatives to capitalism, and Milton's "Areopagitica" suggested the importance of a free press in bringing a new society into being.

In 1922, at the age of fourteen, Stone started the *Progress*, a monthly newspaper he delivered by bicycle after school. By the third issue he had called for an end to Hearst's "Yellow Peril" campaign, support for Gandhi's anticolonialism, cancellation of war debts, and a twenty-five-year international arms suspension agreement. "The paper was printed in the job shop of a local weekly," Stone recalled some fifty years later, "and the linotypist, after setting some of these early radical effusions, opined between meditative squirts of tobacco juice, that I would come to a bad end."

The third issue of the *Progress* was the last. Bad grades in high school caused the Feinsteins to exercise parental censorship on their young Milton. But the next year, Stone was allowed to take an after-school job with the Camden (N.J.) *Evening Courier*, then owned by J. David Stern, who would later employ Stone at the Philadelphia *Record* and the New York *Post*. While Stone learned the basics of newspaper work, he also entered his only period of partisan political involvement. He joined the New Jersey Socialist Party and was elected to its executive committee before he was old enough to vote. Though sympathetic to Al Smith, Stone did publicity work for Norman Thomas in 1928 (as a teenager he had supported Senator Robert M. LaFollette's Progressive Party presidential candidacy in 1924). Stone was later to write that he abandoned party politics because he "felt that party affiliation was incompatible with independent journalism." But there was more to it than that. Stone was even then putting together a world view that would combine belief and practice in a way that would be comfortable and consistent, but also uniquely right for him. His reasons for supporting Thomas some fifty-five years ago point also to his own personal development: "I immensely admired his capacity to deal with American problems in Socialist terms but in language and specifics that made sense to ordinary Americans."

Stone has said he felt uncomfortable with left-wing politics because of the sectarianism of the Left. But this feeling may be a retrospective explanation. By quitting the University of Pennsylvania in his junior year, and beginning his full-time career as a newspaperman at twenty, Stone avoided the academic life that fostered so much of American left-wing partisanship. Stone chose very early on to go it alone, and his long career has been almost entirely free of the radical intellectual bickering that so consumed much of the American Left. Stone's development can also be seen in light of his autodidactism. He was accepted to Pennsylvania only because of an open enrollment provision for area students—he had graduated forty-ninth in a high-school class of fifty-two. He was motivated by both a strong hunger to learn and a sort of "Harvard envy" which, with too great a measure of self-deprecation, made him feel intellectually inadequate.

But Stone was fortunate in his employers. They gave him freedom to say what he thought, and, perhaps more important, time to develop his special blend of philosophical concern and scrupulous attention to detail. While working as an editorial writer, Stone could plunge into a study of Turgot's economic policies under Louis XVI and also brave his way through the thousands of pages of economic proposals and dictates being issued daily by the new Roosevelt administration.

Stone became an editorial writer for the Philadelphia *Record* in 1931 and joined the New York *Post* in the same capacity in December, 1933. As early as 1934, Stone saw the potential link between war and economic recovery. He became convinced that only by expanding executive powers could the

United States pull out of the Depression. After giving himself a crash course in constitutional law, Stone published his first book, *The Court Disposes*, in 1937. He argued that the justices of the Supreme Court had overstepped constitutional bounds on economic issues while at the same time failing to support constitutional protections of civil and political liberties. While the book was not groundbreaking in either its legal or historical analysis, it is important for an understanding of how Stone was influenced by the New Deal. Despite his later disagreements with Roosevelt's policies, FDR would remain the benchmark of Stone's view of the American presidency.

In 1937, fearful that fascism and bitter anti-Semitism might come to the United States, Stone changed his name from Isidor Feinstein, first to Geoffrey Stone and then to I. F. Stone. He later recalled that he "still felt badly about" this change. In 1938, after a series of odd jobs, Stone was hired by Freda Kirchwey as associate editor for the *Nation*. And with his move to the nation's capital in 1940 as that magazine's Washington editor, the I. F. Stone we know today emerged. Though his Popular Front position had made him something of an apologist for the Soviet Union in the 1930s, after the Nazi-Soviet pact he supported the American war effort. He devoted dozens of articles in the *Nation* to revealing how American business was deliberately planning shortages and manipulating scarcity to bolster profits. One of the first to call for government supervision of the wartime economy, Stone published *Business as Usual* to wide attention in 1941. Stone continued to keep a careful eye on business activity under the Office of Price Administration and the War Production Board, exposing the laxity and ineptitude of the businessmen summoned to Washington to monitor themselves. In his memoirs, John Kenneth Galbraith recalls with some amusement how OPA Administrator Leon Henderson went to elaborate lengths to mislead reporters about the nature of an agreement between the OPA and the tire industry. When Henderson finished his statement, Stone shot out, "Mr. Henderson, can we assume that a deal has been cut?"

In 1941, Stone took a second full-time position with Ralph Ingersoll's *PM*, and it is from this period also that much of what Stone was producing as daily and weekly journalism seems today to read like history. His theses on preparedness and the wartime economy were confirmed in studies in the late 1960s and early 1970s. His demonstrations of how the war—and the war only—beat the Depression were appearing as the "discoveries" of revisionist historians twenty years later. Upon Roosevelt's death, Stone, who had by now found his geographic and professional niche, found also his foil—Harry S Truman.

As early as the founding conference of the United Nations in April, 1945, in San Francisco, Stone sensed that the Truman era would be "haunted" by the twin specters of Cold War abroad and suppression of dissent at home. Reading Stone's columns for the *Nation* and *PM*, one recognizes the prescience of a remarkably keen and thoughtful observer. In the first years of Truman's administration, Stone predicted the split among nations on pro- and anti-Soviet lines, the appearance of what he called a "Third Force" of emerging nations, the rebuilding (and eventual re-arming) of Germany and Japan as defenders of "conservative capitalism," the world proliferation of nuclear weapons, and the development of virulent anticommunism in the United States.

In 1946 Stone took a break from his duties in Washington

to chronicle for *PM* the plight of thousands of stateless Jewish refugees from Europe whom the British forcibly repelled from entering Palestine. He was the first journalist to evade the British embargo and report firsthand on the effort to build a Jewish state through armed rebellion. *Underground to Palestine* appeared later that year. Menachem Begin's Irgun even used it as a training manual in their struggle against the British Mandate; and Stone was awarded a medal by the Haganah, but his "AWOL" *PM* assignment ended his *Nation* editorship. (Stone's coffee-table book *This Is Israel* was published in 1948.)

With the closing of *PM*, Stone went to work for its successors, the New York *Star* and then the *Daily Compass*, focusing much of his attention on the House Un-American Activities Committee and on the Korean conflict. As American foreign policy shifted toward containment and military commitment in Korea grew, Stone began asking a series of hard questions without getting any answers. He devoted many of his columns to General MacArthur's duplicity and possible insubordination, and speculated on links between Taiwan's Chiang Kai-shek and South Korean president Syngman Rhee. In 1951 he completed a book-length study, *The Hidden History of the Korean War*. The book remained in manuscript for over a year despite various promises to publish it (including one from Jean-Paul Sartre) until an accidental meeting with Leo Huberman and Paul Sweezy in New York City led to its publication under the new Monthly Review imprint.

On Election Day in November 1952, the *Compass* failed to appear—the venture was bankrupt. Corliss Lamont had foreclosed on the paper's mortgage, and Stone was out of a job. He thought at first of going back to the *Nation,* but several differences with Freda Kirchwey made that impossible for him. Never one to brood, Stone summoned up the spirit of his teenage years and determined to put out his own paper. He decided, too, that he would be the sole proprietor and editorial staff for the new publication. He would be "an independent capitalist, the owner of my own enterprise, subject to neither mortgager or broker, factor or patron . . . a wholly independent newspaperman, standing alone," as he later wrote. He would even have "one up on Benjamin Franklin"—he would accept no advertising.

With $3,500 in severance pay from the *Compass,* a $3,000 interest-free loan from a friend, and the able assistance of his wife, Esther (who would act as business manager for eighteen years) and his brother Marc, Stone began. With the benefit of the mailing lists of *PM,* the *Star,* and the *Compass,* Stone was able to secure 5,300 charter subscribers for his new venture, among them Bertrand Russell, Eleanor Roosevelt, and Albert Einstein. The idea was not altogether new. By Stone's own admission, his inspiration came less from Ben Franklin than from George Seldes, who had published the one-man *In Fact* through the 1940s. *In Fact* was a brash, almost bizarre weekly that crusaded against fascism, the Catholic Church, and the auto, liquor, and tobacco industries. (It was Seldes who first alerted the public to the link between cigarette smoking and lung cancer.) Stone admired more the spirit of Seldes's enterprise than its specific content or style.

The times were inauspicious for radical journalism, and Stone knew it. He determined to present the paper in such a way as to avoid any charges of sensationalism or irrelevance.

"My idea was to make the *Weekly* radical in viewpoint but conservative in format," Stone later recalled. Stone also made an honest assessment of what he could best accomplish on his own. Limited (or so it would seem) by a serious hearing problem, he determined that he would devote himself to ferreting out important information from the mass of hearings, official transcripts, and government documents that were the ticker tape of Washington. He had trained himself during his years with the *Nation* and *PM* in the techniques of analyzing these diaries of bureaucracy. But now he would also be free to merge these facts with his own philosophy: "I felt that if one were able enough and had sufficient vision, one could distill meaning, truth, and even beauty from the swiftly flowing debris of the week's news." He also would use style and wit, both of which he had in abundance. "I dreamed of taking the flotsam of the week's news and making it sing," he recalled in his last issue.

Stone was supremely adept at reading the nation's newspapers, something he demonstrated was not as easy as most newspaper readers—or publishers—might think. He once told David Halberstam that the Washington *Post* was "an exciting paper to read because you never know on what page you would find a page-one story." And this was Stone's goal: to find the page-one stories, week after week, wherever they might be. He was looking for what Galsworthy "in another context called 'the significant trifle'—the bit of dialogue, the overlooked fact, the buried observation which illuminated the realities of the situation." One light example: during the Lebanon crisis of 1954, Stone spotted in the *Congressional Record* a lecture by Speaker Sam Rayburn to

Congressman Henry Reuss regarding Reuss's opposition to dispatching the marines: "In times like these we had better allow matters to develop rather than make remarks about them."

But the *Weekly* was filled with more than such one-liners. Stone was able to document official lies about McCarthyism, the Dominican Republic, Vietnam, the civil-rights movement, and numerous other subjects; and out of these accumulated observations he was able to assemble the truth. "The bureaucracies put out so much that they cannot help letting the truth slip from time to time," he noted. By carefully following Indochina from 1950 onward, Stone knew all the players well enough to spot the inconsistencies and outright lies behind Lyndon Johnson and Robert McNamara's direction of American involvement in Vietnam. Stone devoted his August 24, 1964, issue to "What Few Know about the Tonkin Bay Incidents," a lonely journalistic defense of senators Wayne Morse and Ernest Gruening's defiance of Johnson's Tonkin Gulf Resolution. Stone documented Johnson and McNamara's deceptions within weeks of their occurrence. Four years later, the New York *Times*, the Washington *Post*, and CBS News would begin to announce the same findings as "exclusives."

His first issue, which appeared a few days before Eisenhower's inauguration, contrasted the Cold War gloom of Truman's last State of the Union speech with the statesmanship and tolerance of George Washington's Farewell Address. Nevertheless, while calling for a commutation of the death sentences of Julius and Ethel Rosenberg, Stone saw fit to contrast the relative attention to procedure and the rule of law in the Rosenberg case with the total sham of the "doctors' trial" then in progress in the Soviet Union. By the spring, the *Weekly* had subscribers in all forty-eight states, as well as Alaska, Hawaii, Puerto Rico, Latin America, Western *and* Eastern Europe, and Israel. Stone reached 10,000 readers by 1955 and 20,000 by his tenth anniversary in 1963. Real growth in readership came as Stone emerged as an essential guide to the politics behind the Vietnam War: 40,000 in 1968; 50,000 in 1969; 60,000 in 1970; and over 70,000 by the final issue in December, 1971. Stone never raised the subscription rate of $5 a year, and the paper never changed in format or purpose. Publication was suspended briefly, however, in 1968 after Stone suffered a heart attack and it went to biweekly after his return. His last issue was devoted to an autobiographical reminiscence, but the *Weekly*'s penultimate number detailed the narrow constitutional and civil-rights view of the newly nominated Supreme Court justice, William H. Rehnquist. In the *Weekly*'s last year, Stone received one of journalism's most prestigious prizes, the George Polk Memorial Award—the same year that Walter Cronkite was similarly honored for the CBS documentary "The Selling of the Pentagon." After closing the paper, Stone continued to contribute to the *New York Review of Books* and other publications. (He had written the first essay on Vietnam to appear in the *Review*—back in 1964.) He made a brief effort with a syndicated column in 1980, but has devoted the bulk of his time to ancient Greek—for several years in the late 1970s as Distinguished Scholar in Residence at American University.

Stone is a unique figure in American journalistic history, never content to be either a "straight" reporter or a partisan polemicist. Barred officially and unofficially from the major media, he remained free to speak and write his mind. And he was disciplined enough to establish a consistent style and format, and good enough to earn a reputation for accuracy and honesty. It seems doubtful that there is a writer today with the skill and patience, the reporter's instincts, the wit and style, and the dedication to ideals older and more durable than the latest left-wing trend, that would be needed to start the presses on a worthy successor to *I. F. Stone's Weekly*.

I really have so much fun, I ought to be arrested. Sometimes I think it's wrong of me, because, you know, if you're a newpaperman, as I've been since I was fourteen years old—to have your own little paper (it may be very small; as Daniel Webster said about Dartmouth, "It may be a small college, but there are those that love it")—to be able to spit in their eye, and do what you think is right, and report the news, and have enough readers to make some impact, is such a pleasure, that you forget, you *forget* what you're writing about. It becomes like—you're like a journalistic Nero fiddling while Rome burns, or like a small boy covering a hell of a big fire. It's just wonderful and exciting and you're a cub reporter and God has given you a big fire to cover. And you forget—*that it's really burning!**

* I. F. Stone speaking in the film *I. F. Stone's Weekly*, by Jerry Bruck, Jr., 1973.

3

SOCRATES ET AL.

"I'M WORKING on this book on the trial of Socrates. It started out with the idea to be a study of the problem of freedom of thought. Not freedom, which has a lot of ambiguities to it—but freedom of thought and expression. And I started by spending a year on the English Seventeenth Century Revolutions, and I had a fascinating time. And then I felt that I couldn't understand the English Seventeenth Century Revolutions without understanding the Reformation. When I got to the Reformation, I felt that I had to understand the premonitory movements that began in the Middle Ages. When I got there, I felt I had to understand the classical period.

"When I got to the classical period, I thought I would be able to do a cursory survey based on standard sources. And I discovered that there really were no standard sources and everything was controversial, and I discovered that I couldn't make valid philosophical or political inferences from a translation. Not because the translators were incompetent and I was better, but because the words are rarely congruent. You understand what I mean by congruent? Did you have plane geometry? You know: when two triangles are congruent their territory is the same. So the translator is forced to choose among a number of different possibilities, and he's always up against a terrible problem: Does he translate the same Greek word the same way throughout the translation, or does he use different words? If you use the same word, it leads to great confusion. If you use different words, it's equally confusing without an explanation. And if you don't know the language then you really have to use—sometimes I think *nobody* knows Greek, but certainly *I* don't, but I've made progress—you have to use more than one translation, or trot, because otherwise you think that this is the only way to translate it. When you use other translations by equally good scholars you begin·to get the full dimensions of possibilities of the word.

"So I began to—I'd had six years of Latin and only one semester of Greek before I quit college. (I had four years of Latin in high school.) So I began to brush up enough to use a bilingual edition and look up the crucial conceptual terms in the lexicon. Then I began to memorize—if I had realized how far I was going to be drawn, I would have gone back to school. But then I didn't realize how far I was going to go. Then I began to conjugate and to learn declensions. And then I read the Gospel of St. John, which is easy. Then I went to the other end of the Greek language cycle and read the first book of the *Iliad* and then I went on and I've read just about all of Plato, paying attention to the text as well. I spent four months on the *Apology of Socrates*. It is *beautiful*! He's a great artist. And that's one reason he survived.

"I've often said that nobody has ever gotten away with so much egregious nonsense out of sheer charm as Plato. It's nonsense—absolute nonsense. And the devout Platonists—it's like a cult, they're like Moonies. I mean, Plato is a fascinating thinker, and a marvelous writer, and a man of comic genius. Olympiodorus says that he wanted to be a writer of comedy, of plays and comedy—he's supposed to have had a copy of Aristophanes on his bed when he died—but when he met Socrates he gave that up. And he contributed some very, very important insights to philosophy. But in philosophy, I think, almost any insight, if carried too far, particularly systemized, becomes nonsensical. And so you have to take each philosopher for what he contributes. And you have to read him, too, not just for his system or ideas, but for the way he gets at it, for all the by-products, the joy, and the wrestle, so to speak. No other philosopher turned his philosophy into little dramas. That gives them part of their continual charm. Some of them are very, very beautiful. The *Phaedo* is just—I was reading the *Phaedo* at American University, and I came to the end. I just burst into tears. The kids must have thought I'd gone wacky. It's very moving. A great drama.

"And then when I got back to the ancient world, I was so angered by the trial of Socrates—as a civil libertarian, and as a lover of Athens, the first great city. How could it have happened? So I got stuck. And to understand the trial, well, I went back to Rome. (In the meantime, I was reading Greek poetry and Homer and I'm on my eleventh play. The plays are very hard, as you probably know.) And I began to read Latin again. Because I find that on any point, if there were only one thing in the universe, it would be incomprehensible. Because if you look more closely at the problem of comprehension, it all boils down to comparison and contrast. And if you had nothing to compare it with, nothing to contrast it with, it would be ineffable. So I find that at any point in Greek studies, if you go to the kindred civilization of Rome, and study that same aspect, the comparison, especially the contrast, is very illuminating.

"And so, you understand the Greek theater and its wellsprings of freedom much better when you look at the Roman theater and comedy. And with the Greek law and the Roman law, the procedure and laws of the Greek Assembly and the Roman Assembly, it's very, very fascinating. I don't care much for Rome. Cicero is a big tub of crap. Typical corporation lawyer and ass-kisser of the rich and powerful. But he studied in Athens, a few centuries after the great days, and his philosophical treatises, while they're not profound, are very valuable. You consult what he has to say in the *De natura deorum*, *De divinatione*, and the *Tusculan Disputations*. And then I read his two essays, the *De amicitia* and *De senectute*—they're beautiful. I agree with Caesar, though. He called the prose style Asianic, by which he meant overadorned, and I think his speeches are a little bit too flowery.

"And, of course, Cicero and Plutarch were the two great transmitters of classical antiquity to the modern world, through the Middle Ages. So, in addition, to understand the issues, I found myself running up and down the centuries: going from the *Nicomachean Ethics* to look in St. Thomas Aquinas to see what he had to say about it, studying Nicholas of Cusa to see how he interpreted things—he's a wonderful figure, by the way. I just read my first Medieval Latin, the *De pace fidei* of Nicholas. Nicholas's doctrine was the unknowability of God, which is also in

Philo Judaeas and elsewhere. But his particular form of it—
he anticipated the calculus. He used the polygon and the
circle—and the tangent and the curve—to explain the un-
approachability of God. And from this he inferred religious
tolerance. He was a Roman Catholic cardinal, and his *De
pace fidei* is a discussion in Heaven with St. Peter presiding.
And you have a Jew, a Muslim, a Greek Christian, Hus-
sites, all disputing. It's never been translated into English
and the Medieval Latin is very hard, and there's no real
lexicon. This is because Medieval Latin, like Yiddish, was
affected by every country in which it was spoken. So there's
always an interlay of native words. So, for example, in
Rashi, a French Jew, there are French words in his Hebrew.
And there's no lexicon of *philosophical* Latin. The Greek-
English lexicon stops with the fifth century A.D. The English are rather sniffy about the Middle Ages, anyway.
The new enormous Latin lexicon brought out in England
doesn't even go *as far as* the fifth century A.D.!

"I found in the Library of Congress a modern German
translation of Nicholas, so the German trot helped me to
understand the Latin. Have you ever read Ernst Cassirer's
Individual and the Cosmos in Renaissance Philosophy? It's a
wonderful book, and about a third of it deals with Cusa.
It deals with the Platonic Revival in Florence. Nicholas was
the last papal legate of Constantinople before it fell to the
Turks. And he was one of those who brought back the
Platonic texts thitherto unknown in Western Europe.
Western Europe knew only the *Timaeus* in an abridged Latin
translation up until about the Tenth or Twelfth Century.
Then they knew the *Meno* and one other, I forget which

25

one. But they didn't know most of it. Most of Platonism came from Dionysius the Areopagite. And in a thing like the *Theaetetus*, the question of definition was so important to Socrates, I found myself in Wittgenstein. You know anything about Wittgenstein?

"So the issues are living—philosophical, political. You run up and down the centuries. I do three lectures on the trial of Socrates. One on "What Plato Doesn't Tell Us"— except by indirection. The second on how easily Socrates could have won acquittal, without humiliating himself. See, I don't defend the verdict, at all, of course! And three, I put Plato on trial, see what he would have substituted for the great city of Athens. So while these deal, very intensively, with the trial, they become a kind of mini-introductory course on classical antiquity. They bring together insights from the whole of antiquity.

"Of all the other *Apologies* besides Xenophon's and Plato's, they've all disappeared except for that of Libanius. Libanius is very interesting because he alone argues the case the way I would have argued it: as a civil libertarian. Very strange that in a city as devoted to free speech as Athens was that Socrates never pleads the case for free speech. He pleads *his* right to speak, as the superior man. So I said to myself, if they really had a passion, if they thought of free speech not as a habit but as a principle, they'd have a word for it. What words *were* there for free speech? Well, I discovered there was *no* word for freedom of speech in Rome where there *was* no freedom of speech. But in ancient Athens, there were *four* different terms. And just when I was getting started in all of this I was asked to do a lecture on classical studies at Princeton. So I gave myself three months to chase these four terms down through the whole of literature. And then I'd show how, if I had been Socrates's lawyer, how I could've gotten him off. And that's how it all started."

4

THE BOSS

> To four of the five cities where I published news-
> papers, I came as a stranger. I voiced new points
> of view in editorials which were often raucous and
> abrasive.
>
> J. David Stern
> *Memoirs of a Maverick Publisher*

"I FIRST MET LOUIS BOUDIN through his daughter Vera, who
was married to Sidney Cohen, with whom I went to college
at the University of Pennsylvania. It was very lonesome
being an intellectual in a very small *Main Street* town. In fact,
we lived on Main Street! What Sinclair Lewis described was
not very different from my town. If you were a bookworm,
a radical, an intellectual . . . I still remember the day I discovered Christopher Marlowe in the library when I was a
sophomore in high school. I still have a visual memory of
that Mermaid Classics edition—the yellow binding with the
gold letters—and beginning to read all that wonderful bom-
bast in *Tamburlaine*. I read a lot of the Elizabethans. When I
went to college, I met a whole gang of young, Jewish, New
York intellectuals. One of them was Sidney Cohn. That's
how I got to know Louis and [his nephew] Leonard. Leonard
and I married sisters. Louis was a great Marxist scholar. His
book on the theoretical system of Karl Marx is one of the
things I read. And there's his wonderful book on the Supreme

29

Court, *Government by Judiciary*. One of my most painful moments was when Sidney didn't have money to get back to New York once, and I had had a two-volume edition of Dyce, a famous mid-Victorian Elizabethan scholar—his edition of Beaumont and Fletcher and [laughs] it still breaks my heart to think of it—I sold it to help him raise train fare to get back to New York.

"My book [*The Court Disposes*, 1937] had a peculiar origin. I think it was through Sidney I was asked to talk to a labor union being formed at Macy's. This was in the thirties under the New Deal, and I was editorial writer at the New York *Post*, and they wanted a talk on the Supreme Court controversy—it was before the president's [court-]packing plan. I had begun doing a lot of reading in constitutional law, because all of the New Deal reforms were being thwarted in the court. Even earlier, when I first became editorial writer on the Philadelphia *Record*, just before Roosevelt came in, we were calling for a state income tax, and the attorney general of Pennsylvania, Schnader, said it would be unconstitutional because it would violate the uniformity clause of the Constitution. That was the beginning of my constitutional-law studies. I studied the whole problem and argued that it was nonsense on his part. That was my first taste of the pleasures of constitutional law. It was a lot of fun.

"So when the court began to invalidate New Deal legislation in 1935, I read every decision every week in the advance sheets. And then my boss, David Stern, was invited to a dinner with three great scholars—very famous in that time. One was Edward Corwin of Princeton. One was John Dickinson, who was then assistant attorney general in the antitrust division and had been lawyer for the Pennsylvania Railroad, a real juicy job. The third was Dean Goodrich of the University of Pennsylvania Law School. And the editorial writers were invited, three of us. Stern had the Camden *Courier*, the *Record*, and the New York *Post*, and editorials were shared. (When Stern bought the *Post*, he took me up there in December of thirty-three.) We were afraid that these guys were going to talk the boss out of our very critical treatment of Supreme Court decisions. I tried to be critical within the framework of constitutional law, not just write demagogically.

"So I boned up for that dinner as if I was boning up for an examination. I went back to the conciliar controversy in the Middle Ages within the Catholic Church, where the concept of a higher law started—from which constitutionalism derives—and of course Aristotle has that same conception, when he discusses the *Antigone*; and it's in Sophocles. In the western world later, I think the first beginning of the constitutional idea is when you're subjecting the popes to the councils—to that higher law. And then I just worked my way down.

"They treated us rather pompously. Dickinson had a big belly with a heavy watch chain. He looked like a caricature of a corporation lawyer, which is what he was—but a very great scholar; I later got to be very friendly with him. I never agreed with him on anything, but he was tremendously learned in the law and in American history. And at one point the conversation turned to the Privileges and Immunities clause, and one of the writers said it hadn't been used. And I popped up and I said, 'No, last week, last Tuesday, in the Vermont tax case [*Colgate* v. *Harvey*, later overruled], the Supreme Court for the first time utilized the Privileges and Immunities clause in a way analogous to the due-process provision.' And when I contradicted—I think it was Corwin—my boss looked at me as if to say, 'Izzy, for God's sake shut up! You're with experts!' I was a brash sonofabitch as a kid . . . And Dickinson backed me up and Dickinson leaned back and he said 'Why, Ned! He's in our field, Ned. He's in our field.' [Laughs.] My moment of triumph! So that consolidated me with Stern— I was the guy that handled constitutional issues on the paper.

"But then we had a fight that led eventually to my loss of a job. In 1939, he wanted an editorial written—there was a strike at a Brooklyn department store. There was secondary picketing, and he wanted me to write an editorial saying that it was unconstitutional. And I said, 'Look, the Supreme Court recently upheld secondary picketing. I can't write that!' So he was really sore. 'Goddammit, I need that editorial to get the department-store advertising.' And I said, 'Goddammit, why didn't you tell me that in the first place? I've been in a whorehouse long enough to know what one's supposed to do! You tell me to write it, I'll write it—but don't give me an argument that I know isn't true!' I don't think I ever wrote the editorial. But it was a lot for the boss to take, because he really was an idealist—and he hated to have to compromise. He didn't mind being contradicted. I was fighting with him right from the beginning and we were good friends.

"My relationship with him went back to when I had my little paper, the *Progress*, for three months in Haddonfield— and my father made me stop it. I got a job on the local *Public Press*. The next year I was a junior at high school, and Stern came around to our store one night and said, 'I heard about you. Would you like to be my Haddonfield correspondent?' I said, 'Yes—sure!' So, this was an important district, Haddonfield, from the circulation point of view. And Harry T. Saylor, the managing editor, took one look at me, a little Jewish boy in thick glasses and knee pants!—I was fifteen—and he thought, 'Jesus Christ!' He had wanted a man in there, so he felt that he would fire me after a week. Well, the second day of the job, I didn't have any news—and you know it's hard to get news in a small town—and I ran into Mr. Pennypacker of the historical society. He was a leading Quaker and a very nice guy, and I said, 'Look, I'm looking for a story. I'm writing for the *Courier.*' Now, right near our store there was a cemetery. In that cemetery Elizabeth Haddon, the founder of our town, who was celebrated in Longfellow's *Tales of a Wayside Inn*, is buried, but nobody knows exactly where. There's a buttonwood tree and there's a plaque. Mr. Pennypacker said, 'That plaque is in terrible condition, and we'd like to raise some money to fix it up.' Would I like to write a story about it? I said sure. But then on my way home I thought, 'Gee whiz, this is not going to be an easy one!' So . . . I diddled it up a bit. I wrote a story about how an elderly gentleman who had been campaigning to raise money to fix up the plaque was horrified one night when he thought he saw the ghost of Elizabeth Haddon try to polish it up. Now, I didn't write it as straight news—the reader could tell that it was half news and half story—but I sent it in, and I thought, 'My God, it'll get buried. Sure it will.' So after school the next day, I went out and bought the evening paper—it was an evening paper—and there it was atop of page one with a two-column head and a byline. They gave me a bonus and ten cents an inch, so it came out to forty-five cents an inch for that story!

"I used to go into Camden with news, write it in the

office, and then ride home on the trolley car with Dave Stern, the publisher, late at night. He was so sleepy, he'd fall asleep, and part of my job was to shake him up at the end of the car line. His wife was a wonderful woman and a friend. I had the run of their library. She was very much of a bookworm, and a graduate of Bryn Mawr. I had been reading modern poetry at first—Carl Sandburg, Edgar Lee Masters, and things like that. And there I began to read Keats and Shelley.

"I always wanted to be a newspaperman. The year before he gave me the job—after my father made me give up my paper—I heard there was a job open covering sports at our high school at the *Post-Telegram*, the opposition paper to Stern, so I called them up. And they said that there was a big basketball game, would I cover it? I was a non-sports kid. I got there in the middle of the game, at the half, and I began by asking, 'What's the object of the game? Show me what they do. What are the goals? Was there anything dramatic?' And I wrote a very good story—very colorful, full of crap, and so I had a job as a sportswriter. The only time I worked as a sportswriter. So I'd already had my own paper, worked for the *Public Press* weekly in Haddonfield, and as a correspondent for Stern's opposition. So I would have gone that way anyway. But it was wonderful to work for him, because he was a good antifascist and he did a lot of exposé journalism. He was a real muckraker, and he believed in investigative journalism, and he made circulation with it. And he had a very liberal editorial policy. In the 1924 campaign, when the paper was nominally Republican, it was the only paper in the whole Philadelphia area that wrote respectfully about LaFollette and Wheeler's Progressive Party.

"Later, we had a falling out. The paper was in a very bad way, and I guess he didn't want to fire me, he'd have to pay me an awful lot of severance pay so he demoted me to reporter. I'd been an editorial writer for about seven or eight years, beginning in Camden. But I was a good reporter. Much to his surprise—much to everybody's surprise—I just had one hell of a good time in the newsroom, and the first day, I got a page-one story. It was fun to be back on the street covering stories. Everybody looked at me askance, I was the fair-haired boy and here I was demoted. Then they caught on that I was having too much fun, so they stopped giving me general assignments. Charles Evans Hughes was about to die so they set me up to prepare an obituary. So I went to the library, I had all this time at my command, I read everything Charles Evans Hughes did on the Supreme Court, both when he'd been an associate justice before the First World War and the ten years when he'd been chief justice up to that time. But Hughes didn't die, and they would just keep me sitting there. So I did pieces for the Nation. And then I brought a Guild case for my severance pay, arguing that my demotion was constructive discharge, and Francis Biddle was the impartial arbiter, and he ruled for my boss. So, when I lost, I left. I did some odd jobs for a while. I wrote an investors' paper for a while for an investors' union, like Consumers Union, a muckraking investors' paper, and I wrote some financial columns for the *Nation*.

"And then in September, 1939, I gave up a job for $250 a week as a speech writer for Lawrence Tibbett in his struggle against Petrillo, the gangster leader of the musicians' union. It was the highest paying job I'd ever had. In those days, that was a lot of money. But Freda Kirchwey offered me a job.

"She'd first offered me the Washington job in 1938. She said there was a new job open as a press officer for the Interior Department, and then I could work for her on the side. I said no. Even though I agreed with the New Deal, I didn't want to be a press agent *and* an independent journalist. But then in 1939, she offered me $75 a week and a $10 expense account, and I gave up the $250 and came down here. But I already had three children, and I couldn't make out on that. So I began to do stuff on the side for *PM* and the Washington *Post*, too. So then, in 1941, *PM* gave me a full-time job. So from 1941 to 1946, I had two full-time jobs.

"I had been reading *Nation* and *New Republic* since I was about twelve years old. It was part of my political education. My mother took us to a little summer resort in a little town in south Jersey, and the people that ran it had children who were intellectuals. Their daughter was a good friend of Felix Frankfurter. And on their library table I found, for the first time, *Nation* and *New Republic*. So whenever I'd go to Philadelphia with my mother, she'd buy them for me.

"But Stern was a joy to work for, a joy to work for. You could talk back to him. I'd seen him . . . we had a mechanical superintendent, Elmer Pratt, and I'd seen Pratt bawl the boss out right in front of the whole newsroom. We got some new presses and they weren't working right and Stern finally rolled his shirt sleeves up and went out to the press room and fixed them. He was very informal and very likable. He came of 1848 German stock. But unlike a lot of German stock—I've told you about Macy's? We went to New York, and Sam Untermeyer was our lawyer. Sam was organizing the anti-Nazi boycott. In the twenties, despite the fact that we had a lot of Italians in Camden, the *Courier* was antifascist, and I had read a lot of stuff, people like Salvemini, and I got acquainted with quite a few of the exiles—and then, of course, I followed the rise of Hitler very closely, beginning in twenty-nine and thirty. I remember one German-Jewish reader coming to me, about thirty-one or thirty-two. He said, 'Why are you writing these editorials against Hitler? I got a letter from Germany that says he's only against *Ostjuden*.' . . . And we were the only paper in New York that was really sympathetic to the Spanish Republic. The church was exercising a lot of influence there.

"We were supporting the boycott of Nazi goods, and Macy's—owned by Jews, the Straus family—was selling Nazi goods. Now, department-store advertising was not just revenue, it was also circulation, because women bought the evening paper to see the ads. You didn't have the department-store ads, it was hard to get people to buy the paper. Macy's was the bellwether—if you got Macy's, you could get the others. But Macy's wouldn't come in, because we were on the boycott issue. I remember, about thirty-seven or thirty-eight, there was a peace meeting arranged between my boss and Percy Straus, and everything looked peaceful and he was going to get the ads, and then Percy brought up the boycott—out of the blue—and he said, 'David, how about those editorials?' [Suddenly Stone was silent and seemed quite distracted. I was afraid that he had become ill. Then I realized that he was crying.] You know, as I talk about it, I relive it—these were very hot issues . . . And Stern jumped up and grabbed Percy Straus by the throat. That was the end of the peace meeting. And later he lost the paper, the *Post*. One reason he had to give up the paper, and why Dolly Schiff was able to buy it in thirty-nine, was that he just couldn't get the department-store linage. That was a very honorable thing. And then, of course, there was the Philadelphia strike. I must say, I was a charter member of the Guild. When Heywood Broun came down from New York to Philadelphia to organize the Guild, I joined up. Still, it is true that the Guild was asking things of Stern, who was friendly, that they weren't asking the Philadelphia *Inquirer* which was unfriendly and antiunion. It was sad. He felt hurt about it as a liberal. As a genuine liberal. And also, he was a very paternalistic publisher. Suddenly it was hard for him to be treated like a capitalist boss. There were emotional problems that played a part. I think the Guild was rather unfair in their treatment of him. But I was in New York by that time. It was one of the great pleasures of my life to work for him."

5

POPULAR FRONT

I am not greatly impressed when I. F. Stone finds Russians "browbeaten" because they will not chatter with him as freely as he desires. Russians learned vigilance in a hard school till it became second nature. They will not even abolish "repressive safeguards" until they are sure it is "safe" . . .

I will borrow from my own experience. One reason that I never attacked the USSR for the injustice I suffered was that in a deep sense I felt I had it coming. For years, I had seen scores of people, even my close friends, sent off to Siberia, unjustly. While I protested here and there to officials, I made no outcry to the world. Why then could I protest when the same injustice came to me? Then I asked: *Why* had I made no outcry? And my answer was: Because all those years I felt myself in the presence of something so vast, so important for all men's future, that it must not be halted or diverted whatever the cost. If this was how I decided about others, then thus must I decide about myself.

I think that is what the Soviet people decided. My best woman friend, a professor of English, was exiled for ten years for being "the wife of an enemy of the people," though she was never told the nature of her husband's crime. I met her again after nine years, in Moscow; she had lived as a teacher in a small town in Kazakhstan. Once a month she reported to an officer of the GPU and had "very interesting discussions" with him. He specially pried into her attitude towards her own sentence. Once her reply was, "When a railway train starts going places, what is the attitude of a fly brushed off by the wheel?"

> Anna Louise Strong
> "Critique of the Stalin Era"
> *Monthly Review*, July–August 1956

I don't trust Izzy Stone, Malcolm Muggeridge, Conor Cruise O'Brien, not because of their political position, but because of their methods.

If Izzy says on page 537 of such and such a book you'll hear that so and so . . . I won't believe it. I'll check myself. I don't think he's an honest controversialist. We had to check him every inch of the way when I was at *New Masses* in 1938–39, and just because of the Soviet-Nazi pact. He was more indignant about that pact than anyone I knew. His indignation didn't last long. He was a Stalinist—a loose and nasty term—but by my lights he was. It's not so much being a Stalinist as using their polemical techniques. . . . Izzy's scholarship is impeccable, but based on a load of crap.

> Richard Rovere
> quoted in Philip Nobile
> *Intellectual Skywriting: Literary Politics
> and The New York Review of Books*, 1974

The way home from Moscow has been agony for me. . . . I feel like a swimmer under water who must rise to the surface or his lungs will burst. Whatever the consequences, I have to say what I really feel after seeing the Soviet Union and carefully studying the statements of its leading officials. *This is not a good society and it is not led by honest men.*[original emphasis]

No society is good in which men fear to think—much less speak—freely. I don't care how many tons of steel the Russians produce. It is not by the volume of its steel but by the character of the men it produces that a society must be judged. The kind of men Russia has produced is the kind which must always be wary, quick to sense any change in the wind and adjust to it, careful never to give way to the anguish of seeing injustice, always guarding one's tongue, alert to survive at whatever cost to one's neighbor . . .

What one [sees] is that somehow the attack on Stalin has the same crass, crude air as Stalin's own attacks on his own victims. Stalin had a series of scapegoats on whom he blamed the abuses of his regime in his periodic relaxations. His successors act the same way. Their scapegoat was Beria and then Stalin himself. . . . But to blame the evils of Stalinism on Stalin is obviously inadequate. . . . Stalinism was the natural fruit of the whole spirit of the Communist movement.

But we will not help the Russian people by letting this crowd of leaders soft-soap us; in any free country, after similar revelations, a whole new set of men would have been swept into power as earnest of real change. Nor will we help ourselves, and our power to fight for a better world and a better society, by joining hands with the poor deluded housebroken Communist parties of the West. They remain Russian puppets; they will jump back through the hoops as soon as they get new orders. Their members cannot be freed from intellectual bondage until the parties themselves have disintegrated. Nothing has happened in Russia to justify cooperation abroad between the independent left and the Communists.

I. F. Stone
"The Legacy of Stalin"
I. F. Stone's Weekly
May 28, 1956

STONE DISTINGUISHES HIMSELF from "pure" Marxists: "Paul Sweezy, who's a very sweet person, is an old-fashioned nineteenth-century Marxist reborn. He's not a Communist. But he's been pretty close to them. For example, when Paul came back from Argentina about ten years ago, I said to him, 'Now, Paul, you're a Marxist, you know, in the traditional sense. Tell me, what makes Argentina tick, from a Marxist point of view?' He wasn't able to give me an answer. You know, in many ways, Marxism applies better to Western Europe than it does to Latin America. I don't mean it doesn't apply to Latin America, too. But there's a cultural factor. Years ago when I was on the *Nation*, we used to always talk about getting out a really good book on the State Department. And I used to say that to get a really good book on the State Department, you needed somebody who was a combination of Pearson and Allen of the old 'Washington Merry-Go-Round,' for the inside dope; Marx, for class forces; Weber, for institutional forces; and Henry James, for social nuances and subtleties. Well, with Argentina you have the cultural patterns of the Spanish Conquest and the Spanish heritage of Roman Catholicism at its worst. All these things lay a very deep impress on Latin America. Where else could you have a country settled by West Europeans, very few Indians or blacks, a temperate climate, an excellent constitution based on American and French models, and genuine, sincere lefties who were *Peronistas*? *That* really boggles the mind. Perón himself fits the pattern of Julius Caesar better than he does the pattern of modern fascism. In a sense, like Caesar, he crushed the old patrician class, subdued them, and gave a lot to the lower class to establish his power. It's much more Caesarian in that sense than it is fascist—because the working class won a good deal under Perón and the lower classes won a lot under Caesar."

But Stone does defend Marx and his methods, not so much from attacks from the Right, as from those on the Left who try to categorize contemporary issues and events in neat "Marxist" categories. For Stone, many contemporary leftists are ideologues rather than students of history and society. Stone defends his pragmatism in terms of action as well as theory: he remains an avid proponent of Popular Front concepts. He is dismissive of much of today's "easy" Marxism.

"It's not a genuine Marxism. I mean, Marx is a very close observer. A lot of his works were based on the parliamentary investigations in the press. Which is—I'm not comparing myself—but he used the same raw material I used in the *Weekly*: the bourgeois parliamentarians and the bourgeois press. So did Lenin. You read *State and Revolution*, you'll see how closely Lenin read the establishment press in Switzerland. You see, this whole thing has to be seen in a very important perspective, and that is: one way in which Marx and Engels were mistaken is that, if you look back at the *Manifesto*, they envisaged the proletariat becoming the overwhelming majority of the population. And instead, in none of the advanced industrial countries is the industrial working class the majority. There's a new middle class, and it's impossible to fight fascism without combining the progressive elements of the middle-class parties with the Left against fascism. I mean, that was true in Italy. In Italy in the twenties, I remember it very well, I was very politically aware; there was a basis there for a genuine *apertura sinistra*. And those on the Left—there was a majority there of progressive Catholics and leftist laborites who could have stopped Mussolini. And the same thing was true of Germany. Von Schleicher tried to form what would have been a kind of National Front of anti-Nazi elements in the army and of the upper middle class with the Left, and von Papen pulled the rug out from under him thinking that he, von Papen, could manipulate Hitler, could use Hitler to bring himself to power. It's very murky, a lot of intrigue there. But the basic thing is that you need tactics and programs that can appeal to the progressive elements of middle-class parties—like the Christian Democrats in Chile, for example. That's why Allende never got a majority, unfortunately. He had only a plurality. So that's the philosophical basis for the whole Popular Front idea.

"Whereas, if you had what Marx and Engels envisioned—an iron law of wages and the steady impoverishment of the masses—then two forces would have brought about communism almost automatically. One, the fact that the overwhelming majority of the people were proletarian, and two—this is equally important—that capitalism creates its own antithesis in the sense that the factory system is a collective system and the corporation is a collective system so that both the organization of labor and of capital are collectivized. The internal dynamic of the collective system develops collective forms and the new society, in that Marxian sense, has its embryo in the old. But it didn't work out that way. In fact, it couldn't have worked that way because if you had had a general impoverishment of a majority of the population, to whom would you have sold automobiles, television sets, radios, plumbing? And then, you see, what Marx and Engels talked so contemptuously of, bourgeois democracy—don't forget that when they wrote, democracy in England *was* really bourgeois. The urban working class *and* the rural working class had not yet won the vote. It wasn't until 1867 that Disraeli "dished the Whigs," as he said, and gave the vote to the urban working class; and then, about fifteen years later, the Liberals got their revenge on the country gentry by giving the vote to the rural workers. You had the advantage in England of a ruling class divided between a landed interest and an industrial interest, and some of the great reformers—social reformers, factory reformers—were Tories. That's an experience wholly unlike that of the United States. So, there are all these complexities which don't destroy Marx or the sociology of knowledge, or the class struggle, but they prevent us from—one can very easily take these important insights and apply them in some mechanical and schematic form so that they distort reality instead of illuminating it."

I asked Stone if this wasn't a tragedy of intellectual history: that Marx himself was exempted by his own disciples from the "laws of history" that he had posited.

"*Communist society* is exempt from the laws of history! Just like Hegel figured that the dialectic ended with the Prussian state, Communists figured that the dialectic ended with the Soviet state and the laws of the dialectic don't apply. If you look at the dialectic from the point of view of Heraclitus, who began it—and with great insight—it was the way in which, in one sense, contraries were identical—in one sense. If you don't remember 'in one sense' you go cockeyed. And when you begin to schematize it as the thesis and antithesis and synthesis, you're way away from reality. That's what Hegel added. It was that triadic business.

"Have you read *Memoirs of a Revolutionary* by Victor Serge? He's one of the great moral figures of the age. Romain Rolland and Gide got him out of jail under Stalin, and a lot of the insights of Koestler in *Darkness at Noon* were lifted from Serge. He wrote five wonderful revolutionary novels, including *The Case of Comrade Cure-All*. But his autobiography, the *Memoirs*, is a burning classic of the turmoil of the century. It's agonizing. You see, it was not Marxist to blame everything in Russia on the cult of personality. And it was not Marxist to blame it all on Stalin. If you had Communist friends in the thirties, and just about everybody did, you saw that their whole movement was filled with little Stalins. People like Howard Fast, for example, were petty little dictators. Petty little dictators. They turned your stomach. People like V. J. Jerome were petty little, petty little . . . popes. No other word for them. No, the Popular Front was the right idea. Certainly, the Spanish Republic would have been doomed from the beginning without it."

But was it realistic to think that, over the long term, the Popular Front would have been a successful strategy, given all of these "popes" and the Stalinist tendencies within the Communist movement? What about the examples of the co-opting of non-Communist left-wing parties in Eastern Europe after the war?

"Well, I don't know. I just don't know the answer. I do know that one of the best books on Eastern Europe is by François Fejtel. He was a Hungarian revolutionary in fifty-six, and he fled and he edited that wonderful triple-decker issue of Jean-Paul Sartre's *Les Temps Modernes* that was a symposium of the wall posters, the billboards, the pamphlets of the Hungarian Revolution. And he wrote a book published by the French house "Editions of the Threshold," the publishing house of the theoretical journal of the left Catholics. He was a progressive, not a reactionary. And it may be that some of these regimes might have survived. But they couldn't, he says, once the Cold War started. Each side was so suspicious of the other. Of course, the Russians are really very paranoid. And *we're* really very paranoid. You see, after every great war, the two victors square off against each other for the next war. After the First World War, if you go back and look at history, England and America were the two great powers. The 1922 Naval Disarmament Treaty was an effort to stop the race between them. If there hadn't been the rise of Hitler in Germany, then you might have had very serious trouble between England and America. And when these rivalries start, then propaganda seizes on whatever is bad in the other guy's backyard and draws its whole picture from it.

"There's a wonderful book by the one-time editor of the London *New Statesman*, Kingsley Martin [*The Triumph of Lord Palmerston*, 1924], a study of war propaganda on the eve of the Crimean War, where, for a while, it wasn't known if England and Russia would be together or on opposite sides. And he studied the press and showed that when the two sides were moving toward agreement, you'd have stories about Holy Russia—'the bulbous-towered cathedrals.' And when things moved in the other direction, there'd be a lot of newspaper stories about the Russia of the *knout*. You know that word? A knout is a whip used in Siberia. It's formed by taking a piece of rope and putting lots of knots in it. I think it's a German word, or at least it's cognate with the word *knot*. So Martin showed how the party line of England—how you can take the party line they have in Russia and apply it as an insight into the Western democracies. Because there is in most of them a line of respectable discourse; it's not as rigid as in the Soviet states, not by a long shot, but if you overstep the bounds of respectable discourse to right or left, you're relegated to small publications that live precariously on the edges. The little weeklies and so forth. That's particularly true here.

"But no group likes nonconformists. The tiniest splinter group expels nonconformists. And I *was*—I was *of* the Left, but a *nonconformist* on the Left. And those who were not on the Left, like Rovere, hated me because I was still on the Left; and those in the Left were contemptuous of me because I fell off 'the locomotive of history.' Some of these *ex*-Communists were so *anti*-Communist that they turned against the Popular Front and considered me a fellow traveler, whereas the Communists regarded me as unreliable. Rovere, for example, was an ex-Communist. And ex's have to prove their apostasy."

But how then, I asked Stone, do you build a *society* on the visions of nonconformists, people who can't even put a solid *movement* together?

"It's hard to tell. The bars are never absolute. It's like in science, like in the Catholic Church, the Middle Ages. There's a very good book by Wolfgang Leonhard—teaches at Yale, his mother was a German Communist who fled, about 1937, to the Soviet Union for refuge. She was sent to a camp in Siberia very soon after that, and she got out, about 1949, or maybe a little bit later. And she went to Switzerland and wrote a book in German. I found it in the bookstore once. It was a terrific book called *Elf Jahre im Sovietischen Gefängnis*—Eleven Years in Soviet Prisons. And it's an exposé—boy!—by a Communist. Now, the son was taken away from his mother and educated as one of the elite. And in his book, *Child of the Revolution*, he explains how his disillusion came. This disillusion was very much like that of people in medieval Europe. In other words, you didn't—he didn't—have to read capitalist propaganda. He was disillusioned by the contradictions between 'Holy Writ'—that is between Marx and Engels, even Lenin—and the behavior of the Soviet elite. And in the same way, heretics, heresy, developed in the Middle Ages . . . This guy wants some money . . . "

"God bless you sir! God *bless* you! Thank you!"

"Good luck" Stone says in a singsong voice. "I hate to pass a beggar, because I figure they need to make a certain minimum wage. Even if they're professional beggars! The times are so bad. I see so many more beggars. White and black!" As if on cue, a second beggar approaches. The exchange this time is silent, but Stone's reaction is just as prompt.

"So all of this is like Abelard. I wrote a piece in the New York *Times*, when Andropov came in and clamped down on Roy Medvedev. And I drew a comparison between Medvedev and Abelard—"

"At least Andropov didn't castrate Medvedev!"

"No, but that was a personal matter. Abelard was trying to—was a heretic—and was basically trying to find his way back to the real Christianity, the real Gospel. By the way, did you ever read George Moore's novel *Heloise and Abelard*? It's a wonderful story and it's a beautiful evocation of what life was like in medieval Paris. It is beautiful! Beautiful! Read it some time. But Abelard did a book called *Sic et non*—Yes and no. From deeply respected canonical sources he took contradictory statements about the nature of Christ. It was an eye-opener. Now he didn't dare do that with the Holy Writ, the way Spinoza did later in his *Tractatus theologico-politicus*, where he began the critical reading of the Bible. But with the church fathers, Abelard culled out the contradictions and it was the same for Wolfgang Leonhard in this elite school. People say, 'Those people in Russia don't know what freedom is, they've never had it, so what do they care.' But that's the nature of man: anybody who's a creator, a thinker, an artist, writes to purify his vision and paint it *pure*—not shit. This is the internal dynamics of a society made to break up from within. And I think when you see what a great figure like Pope John XXIII was able to do in the church— he didn't do it as one man. Down below the papacy were all kinds of fresh movements in Catholicism that were really rediscovering the Gospels.

"The Gospels are so radical. You know, when Jesus Christ is in his mother's *belly*, in St. Luke—I read it just recently— she, the Virgin Mary, bursts into a demagogic attack on the rich! I made a speech at the Press Club recently, and somebody said, 'Izzy, how about some prayer in the schools?' I said, 'Look, when I see these terrible deficits, I figure we need all the prayers we can get.' And I said, also, 'Do they know what they're doing, getting kids to pray? Kids might start reading the Bible. Some are even going to become religious!' It's a wonderful book and it's full of wonderful exciting things. And I said, 'You know the saying, "Sooner will a camel pass through the eye of a needle than a rich man enter the kingdom of heaven"? That's not in Karl Marx's *Das Kapital*.' The Bible has been a revolutionary work. So when I see what happened in the church, I figure the same thing: there'll be a new Khrushchev who will go further. Khrushchev was the first liberator. All these dictatorships look so impermeable. Sure, there are Thermidors along the way toward change. And there's John Paul now in the church. The point is, there's a step forward and then a half a step backward. But they don't go back all the way. You compare Russia and China, you don't even get samizdat out of China. And talk about a party line. Here's Joe Alsop writing all this shit about China. Suddenly it's okay to go to China and he and Henry Jackson are right out in the forefront, just like Russian quack-quacks. Just like Russian apparatchiks.

"So, I think some day—all these dictatorships look so goddamned powerful. One day they just collapse. They're rigid, and rigid structures crack. So, I *hope*. Did you ever read Berdyaev's *Origins of Russian Communism*? You should read it. It does for the Russian Revolution what de Tocqueville did in the *Ancien Régime* for the French Revolution. It's a marvelous work. It's a wonderful synthesis of Russian theology, literature, and history by a great Christian mystic of a very pure sort. You know, the czars in the 1890s legalized Marxism as a counterweight to terrorism, and Berdyaev was one of the Legal Marxists. But the Revolution of 1905 failed, and disillusionment followed. He went into the Orthodox Church, and when the Revolution came [1917], he was allowed to go on teaching theology in Leningrad till 1922! Because to some degree he was regarded as a comrade, as a relic of the Legal Marxist movement. So he didn't flee and he wasn't exiled, he was allowed freedom. And he set up a little kind of cult in Paris. But the book, instead of picturing communism as something demoniacal, inexplicable—a kind of Satanic invasion—he shows its deep roots in the Russian past, and the need for revolution to purge all the rotten abuses of the Orthodox Church. Philosophically, he's a real 'anti,' *but* he's a Christian and he sees the Revolution as a kind of spiritual purge of Russia. And instead of saying, 'This is done by the Jews and alien forces,' he shows how deep it runs in the Russian past. It's a wonderful essay. A short book. And a sheer intellectual pleasure to read."

I asked if perhaps some of this tendency on the Left to look for easy categories and automatic analyses hadn't been demonstrated by Czeslaw Milosz in his book *The Captive Mind*.

"I knew Milosz when he was in the embassy here, before he defected. *The Captive Mind* is one of the major, major works. That's the most terrible part of the thing: how intellectuals are destroyed. That happened in the French Revolution too. If you read Anatole France's novel *The Gods Are Athirst*, it's a wonderful picture of the Jacobin character: the contradictions of the idealism, the cruelty, the purity, the horror, all summed up the way it was in the dreadful days of the French Revolution. By the way, Kropotkin wrote a wonderful book on the French Revolution. Have you ever read Kropotkin? He's wonderful—I fell in love with him when I was a boy; when I read *The Conquest of Bread*. He's a pure spirit! Well, I didn't mean to swamp you with all this . . . "

ROUSSEAU

"Rousseau, of whom I don't know too much, seems to me a very half-baked writer who had a great influence. And a deserved influence. But the whole conception of the general will was very much overdone. And the genius of the American Constitution is that it recognizes the general will but not as an absolute power. The right, in the field of ideas, of a single individual or minority is upheld."

6

HOW I GOT THAT STORY

"HAVE I TOLD YOU about how I got my best scoop? It turned out to be a real coup. It'll give you some idea of how I worked and the methods I used to try to cut through all the bullshit that's out there.

"They had the first underground nuclear test in 1957. It really all came out of the screwball mind of Dr. Edward Teller—he's a real Strangelove, maybe *the* real Strangelove—while Stassen was trying to work out a test ban treaty with the Russians. Stassen tried very, very hard as Eisenhower's chief disarmament negotiator—he's a real unsung hero—to get something, but Teller was making the test ban seem unilateral, like some sort of giveaway. As we got close to an agreement, Teller starts to say, 'How can we enforce it? Suppose they go underground? Suppose they go out into space? Suppose they go to the dark side of the moon? We'll never be able to detect them.' And he's got the whole crowd at Lawrence Livermore backing him up on this. They actually got the whole underground test mess going just to try to prove this. They really got us into this terrible miasma.

"So, in the fall of 1957 they had the first test, out in Nevada. Well, of course I wasn't out there, but the next morning in the *Times*, Gladwin Hill's dispatch from the proving grounds said the results seemed to confirm the forecast and expectations of the experts, that it would not be detectable more than two hundred miles away. But the city edition of the *Times*, which I got at home, had a shirttail. You know what a 'shirttail' is? When a paper picks up some information from the wires, related to a larger story, the desk editors will run it as little paragraphs following the paper's own story. They hang down at the end like a shirttail. Well, the city edition had a shirttail from Toronto saying the test had been detected there. When I saw that, I went downtown and got the *late* city, and there were more little shirttails, from Rome and from Tokyo, saying *they* detected it. I didn't have the kind of resources you'd need to cable those places and check out what was happening, but the discrepancy really piqued my curiosity, so I put it away in the basement with my back numbers of the *Times*. I had a real reference library in the basement. You'll see from this how important it was to have these clips.

"The next spring, Stassen testified before Humphrey's Senate Subcommittee on Disarmament that he had got the Russians to agree to listening posts across the Soviet Union every thousand kilometers. A kilometer's about five-eighths of a mile, so he was talking every *620* miles! It would have meant the first lifting of the Iron Curtain. It really looked like a breakthrough for a comprehensive test ban.

"That was on a Tuesday. On Thursday the AEC [Atomic Energy Commission] issued its first official report on that first Nevada test. The AEC was just the worst agency. They were mendacious. They started out right off the bat by telling us that fallout was good for you, and it was all downhill from there. The report was tagged for Monday publication and it said the first test had not been detected more than two hundred miles away. Well they didn't use his name, but they were trying to cut poor Stassen's throat, make a liar out of him and dash the agreement. When I saw the report, I went down in the cellar and dug out the shirttails and called the AEC press office—they had some nice fellas there—and I said, 'How can you guys say this couldn't be detected when the *Times* had reports the next morning that the shot had been recorded on seismographs in Toronto, Rome, and even Tokyo?' 'Izzy,' they said, 'we don't know the answer, we'll see what we can find out and call you back.'

"I wasn't going to just wait for the call. I'd never been on a seismology story before. I figured I better get me a seismologist. I made some calls around town—you see, a scoop isn't a matter of *luck*, you work, you dig, you make calls, you grab the discrepancy, the loose thread, and you pull. And you have to have been paying attention in the first place. That's not *luck*. So my calls led to the Department of Commerce. Their Coast and Geodetic Survey had a seismology branch. I jumped in my car and drove downtown. They were so tickled, they hadn't seen a reporter since Noah hit Mount Ararat, or at least since San Francisco. They showed me their equipment—rather complicated, how to read it, and so forth—and I asked the seismology man if he believed these overseas reports and he said, 'Not really.' But then he said, 'But there are twenty-five of *our* stations'—American stations—'and *they* picked it up.' Well, their stations may just as well have been overseas—I mean, Fairbanks, Alaska, was *2,600* miles away from the test site! And the furthest east, in Fayetteville, Arkansas, was *1,200* miles away. So I said, 'Mind if I jot

these down?' and he said go right ahead. But then he wanted
to know why I was so interested. I told him that the AEC
was going to issue this denial and they looked at each other
and they just clammed up on me. They were scared. They
might have been seismologists but they were still bureaucrats. It didn't matter, I had what I needed and I went
home. I had just walked in the door, when the AEC press
man called: 'Izzy, we heard you were sniffing around at
Coast and Geodetic. It's too late for us to get Nevada on
the teletype, but we'll call you tomorrow. Maybe there's
a mistake.'

"Sure enough, they called Friday and gave me a correc-
tion. But they *didn't* correct their release! I had tipped off
my friend Dick Dudman of the St. Louis *Post-Dispatch*—
that was a very good paper for some time—and he got
them to correct it for him too. But every other paper went
with the AEC lie, making Stassen out to be the fool. Then,
three weeks later, Senator Clinton Anderson, the New
Mexico Democrat, had a special hearing of his Joint Atomic
Committee and asked the AEC chairman, Admiral Lewis
Strauss, 'Wasn't it a story by I. F. Stone that caught you
on this?' And Strauss admitted that it was. It was my great
moment. But it should show you something of how I
worked. The truth slips out from time to time, and enough
of it slips out that there's a piece there for any reporter
who takes the time . . ."

7

GREEK

I REMARKED TO STONE about a professor I knew of who said that he could teach Greek to anyone, and perhaps even within two months.

"I don't know what he means by that. Because, obviously, you could teach certain rudiments quickly. But when you have to apply those rudiments, you come across bewildering problems. For example, I was reading the death of Hector in Homer, to rest up. I've been pretty busy the last few days, a lot of distractions. And I came across the word *enōma*, couldn't figure out what it was, whether it was a noun or a verb. I couldn't find it in the lexicon. I couldn't find it in my lexicon of strange verbal forms. I just couldn't figure out what the hell it was. So finally, I did something that you ought to keep in mind when you tackle Greek. I compared several translations, and figured out that it must be the word for 'ply.' It was Hector plying his knees and legs as he padded like a racehorse across the plain. So I went to my Woodhouse English-Greek dictionary—it's the only one of its kind that I know of—and I looked up the word *ply*. And it gave me a number of different Greek words. Now one of these was the word, a verb, *nōmaō—nu, omega, mu, alpha, omega*—and one of the meanings of that is 'to ply.' So, in a contract verb where you have two vowels together at the end of a verb, the main part, that would be a simple imperfect, the word I'd

59

found, *enōma*. And that didn't rate being put into a dictionary of strange verbal forms, because it's so easy when you have the verb. But I encountered it in an unexpected context, and I just had a *terrible* time with it until I did it backwards, from the trot. And I've often found that useful. I suppose a better scholar than I would have recognized it as a contract verb imperfect. I just wasn't good enough.

"But you know, when I see how great, famous Greek scholars differ violently about certain words in the plays, and particularly in the choruses, I sometimes think it's all Greek to everybody."

8

KOREA

The dominant trend in American political, economic, and military thinking was fear of peace.
General Van Fleet summed it all up in speaking to
a visiting Filipino delegation in January, 1952:
"Korea has been a blessing. There had to be a
Korea either here or someplace in the world." In
this simple-minded confession lies the key to the
hidden history of the Korean War.

> I. F. Stone
> *The Hidden History of the Korean War*
> 1952

"I WROTE THE BOOK in the middle of the war and I haven't
reread it in a long, long time. I think the book really does
three things. One, it raises questions about the origin of the
war that still haven't been answered—I didn't claim to have
the answers. Two, it showed the hostility of the American
military to a truce. And three, it's an exercise in how to study
military propaganda in wartime.

"The book really took its genesis when I was in Paris, in
1950 and 1951, in certain anomalies I noticed in the press:
the discrepancies and contradictions in the communiqués,
particularly around the fall of the southern capital, Seoul. I
had started out believing the official story on the attack of
the North. Why? I just believed it. That's what it looked

like. And in fact, my mission abroad from the paper—then the New York *Daily Compass*, a successor to *PM*—Ted Thackrey, the editor, and I, the chief editorial writer, we regarded the war as an oppression and wanted to bring it to an end. And I went to interview Nehru, in India. Nehru was a neutralist. At that time neutralism was a bad word in both Moscow and Washington. And the paper and I had supported Tito's revolt. So we were in a sort of in-between position, too, and we hoped that Nehru might be able to mediate it. After all, after all the bloodshed and destruction had ended, both sides accepted the *status quo ante* and came back to the 38th parallel. There was enormous suffering, everything above ground was leveled. It was a good little goddamned war.

"I stayed on as a kind of European correspondent in Paris. We lived at Jouy-en-Josas, in Léon Blum's house. And I wrote the book in Paris, and took it to London in the fall. I wasn't able to get a publisher. And in June of 1951, I came back with my family and a manuscript. Those were very bad times. The witch hunt was already on. We came back on the *France*—wonderful—and a big fat immigration official came on board to examine our passports. Passports were then being denied to radicals. And he said in this distinct Brooklyn accent, 'Is youse the Stone that writes for *PM*?' I said, 'Yes, I am.' I thought, 'Oh boy, here's where I lose my passport.' So he stamped it and said, *'Zei gur gezint!'* [Yiddish for 'Go in health!'] It was the most wonderful welcome home! *Zei gur gezint!* So unexpected. Others could not go abroad at all.

"So, one Sunday afternoon I was walking in Central Park—I was working in New York for the paper after we got back—when I ran into Paul Sweezy and Leo Huberman of *Monthly*

Review near the zoo. Huberman and I had worked together on *PM*, and I was always very fond of him. He was a lovely person. A nonacrimonious radical and a wonderful popularizer of economics. His book *Man's Worldly Goods* is an awfully good book. And they said to me something like, 'Do you know anybody who has a good book on the Korean War?' And I said, '*I* got one. Haven't been able to find a publisher.' And they said, 'Well, send it over.' And they took it and then Turnstile Press of the London *New Statesman* took it. The war was still going on when the book was published.

"As a matter of fact, I really wasn't a reader of *Monthly Review*. I wasn't unfriendly to it at all, but I . . . to tell the truth, all through the period when I was writing, I paid very little attention to magazines because I found that in most cases they were really rechewing the same cud that I chewed on from the *daily* papers and then regurgitating it. Of course, when I was in Paris I was reading the French and English press as well. And with the *Weekly*—particularly during the Vietnam War, I read a lot of the Western European press. It was very helpful. I don't mean to say that it was more truthful, but it had a different vantage point. You know what a parallax is? You know, when you measure a star? When you read about the Vietnam War in the French press you had a different viewpoint. It was very valuable because it was a French-language area, and it had been a part of the French Empire. So there was a whole cadre of writers and newspapermen in Paris who had been covering Indochina for a generation. And since it was no longer French after Dien Bien Phu, they could be a little more objective. So people like Phillipe Devillers, a left Catholic, and Jean Lacouture, a left-liberal guy, were real experts. They had been covering the scene since the Second World War, and their analyses were very objective and very good. And they were not party-liners. That is, they weren't willing to echo the propaganda of the other side. And then you had *Le Monde*, *Les Temps Modernes*, and the left Catholic paper, *France Observateur*, for which I wrote some pieces while I was in Paris.

"In fact, the book really grew out of a series of articles I did for the *Compass*. I was doing six pieces a week, that's a lot of work. And it meant that, because they didn't want to spend money on cables, I had to have my stuff at the post office at number 70, rue du Clignancourt, in Paris, by 2 P.M. each day in order to get it to New York the following day. So I was really hopping. And as I became fascinated by the contradictions and other telltale things, I did more and more columns about the Korean War from Paris. So the book was really an outgrowth of the columns. But it was not a paste-up job. And, in my opinion, it was a really well-written book, because it reads like a detective story. It has suspense. Did you find it so? It was not a dull prosy sticking together of clippings.

"Later I heard a funny story from a Polish diplomat who was later purged. A Polish Jew. He told me that my book was being used in the University or in the Foreign Service Training School in Warsaw. This was very interesting to me because it meant that they weren't satisfied with the official propaganda and found my book fresh air. It looked like a more credible account. And then there was the Russian general who defected, the head of the military mission to North Korea. While I was in Paris, he published his memoirs in a right-wing—not a left-wing—French paper. And that gave added credibility to what he had to say. And he revealed that before they went to North Korea, they were instructed not to give the Koreans an air force because they were trouble-makers and they were very wary of them. So you see, coming from a defector, a general in that position, this was very important.

"And history has borne that out. The North Koreans have been a pain in the ass to Moscow and Peking. They're very independent. It's a suffocating dictatorship and its the first example of monarchy in the Communist bloc. I still get the Pyongyang paper. And it is *deadly*. It is the deadliest piece of journalism I've ever seen. And every day, really, there are either two or three stories about how wonderful Kim Il Sung is; and the big fatboy is there being greeted by some obscure official of some obscure African republic, as if he were God Almighty.

"You see, the view here was that this was a deliberate attack by the Soviet Union, through a surrogate, to test our will. But both that series by the Russian in the French press and what the Polish diplomat told me several years later when I was covering the UN indicated to me that Moscow was just as much caught by surprise as was Washington. But it's hard to believe that the *South* provoked the war. Maybe they did, I don't know; but if they *did*, it's very odd that the North was able to get all the way down to the end of the peninsula within a few days. Certainly the South was very badly pre-pared. I was puzzled by that speech that John Foster Dulles had made on the 38th parallel. And I was very suspicious of Dulles, who, I think, is a horrible figure. Nobody liked him at the State Department. He was a hateful person, a real phony. But the way the American military, working with the Korean military, kept upsetting the truce and doing things that made it difficult to have peace was never really spelled out in the American papers the way I spelled it out. And then these peculiar things at the beginning of the war. The book has been billed by people that haven't read it as simply support for the view—for the Soviet propaganda view—that the war was provoked by the South. I don't know, maybe it was provoked. But maybe it wasn't, I don't know.

"Korea and Germany, on opposite sides of the planet, are still tragic flash points that could set the world afire. Microcosmically, they represent, they symbolize, a divided world. And to divide two such energetic and industrious and nationalistic peoples, as the two powers did—they both share the blame—is to prepare the seeds for further trouble. You can still see a lot of further trouble there. On the other hand, the German problem is so difficult, in some ways maybe the best solution *is* to divide the two Germanies. Nobody really trusts the Germans. I don't trust them."

I asked Stone about what appears in his work as an almost obsessive concern with the possible dangers to the world from Germany and Japan. Was this just a legacy of his feelings about the Second World War?

"I don't know. See, when you look into the future, you always look back toward the past for guidance. And there was a great fear that so many people shared—not just myself—that Germany and Japan would rise from the ashes and be a menace in the world. In fact, right now there's more cause for a war between America and Japan than between America and Russia. The American and Japanese relationship in some ways is very much like the English-German relationship before the First World War. If you go back to the literature, at first the British treated the Germans as late and

66

inferior competitors. And pretty soon the British were sore as a boil—they really had a very snotty attitude as tradesmen. They had very good woolens and good steel, and when they went down to South America they said, 'Take it or leave it.' The Germans figured, 'These are warmer countries, they don't need heavy woolens.' They adapted their products to the market, and they were soon outselling the British. Anglo-German commercial rivalry was one of the causes of the First World War. And U.S.-Japanese commercial rivalry is very much like that. I mean we started out by treating them as silly little people that imitated our best products in an inferior way. Now they're really running rings around us. There's a tremendous amount of jealousy. Everybody has it. Even [Jesse] Jackson talks about 'Why don't they defend them-selves?' But who wants a reborn—who wants a rearmed Japan?

"You know, the Western powers saw Hitler as a bulwark against the Soviet Union, a 'bulwark against Bolshevism.' That was a big line. In a sense, Japan has won by peaceful means that 'co-prosperity sphere' that was one of their war aims. They have a dominant position in the Far East, though not quite. Not the position they would have had as a military overlord. It's not just an arithmetical problem: if they build arms, it means you revive an officer caste, you revive the tradition of the samurai. Germany and Japan are very much alike in being latent capitalist countries, late industrial coun-tries, developed countries that still had a feudal overhang, so that the landed warrior aristocracy, the Junkers and the sam-urai, were still the social model even as the bourgeoisie and the capitalists became powerful. So it's very serious. It just shows you that we did a very good job in Japan in many ways. It's the one place where America did a good job after the war. Without a doubt. In remolding the country, we didn't want to recreate the old Japan. This is a very aggressive country. The United States and Russia are countries without a military caste and military tradition—even in the old days in Russia, before the Revolution. And the Russians and Americans have expanded 'peacefully,' pretty much—at the expense of Indians and Asian tribes. Whereas war for the Germans and the Japanese was a cult and a poem and an intoxicant. I felt that then, and I still feel that today.

"In a way it's a shame that we converted the Brussels Pact into the NATO Pact. The Brussels Pact was the Western European powers without Germany as protection against *both* Germany *and* Russia. We stepped in and converted it into NATO. And I think we missed a great—we missed the boat when Stalin offered, I think it was in the early fifties, a reunited, disarmed Germany. It might have been a good deal. It would have prevented East-West tension. On the other hand, we'd have had a united Germany, and that might have been a real headache for both powers."

9

GREEK FREEDOMS

THERE ARE MANY who see the First Amendment to the U.S. Constitution, which explicitly codifies freedom of speech, as providing an absolute protection unknown in the ancient world. Stone rejects this view. He considers free speech to have been at its height in ancient Athens.

"I don't agree with that interpretation, and in my lectures I try to call attention to why I disagree. Number one, the words for freedom of speech in Greek: they had four words for it. And these words represented the fundamental law of Athens. And the Athenians had the *graphē paranomōn,* a legal right to attack a law on the grounds that it was contrary to the fundamental law. And if the Assembly, after hearing the debate, agreed with you, the sponsor of the law could be fined. Now, I call attention to the fact that after the terrible experience with the Macedonians, and with this philosopher-king Demetrius of Phalerum, who ruled Athens for ten years as an absolute ruler under Cassander, king of the Macedonians, they passed a law regulating the teaching of philosophy. It was a law to have no philosophy school whose teaching was contrary to the democracy of the city. And it was passed; but within a year it was attacked in the *graphē paranomōn.* And the Assembly, after hearing the case, upheld the attack, and the schools of philosophy were reopened and lasted until the fifth century A.D. without interference. So you did have a conception of what we would call constitutional law. It wasn't as well developed as in later periods, but you had it.

"For example, Polybius, in discussing the Constitution of the Achaean League says that the real reason for its survival and strength was the fact that there was *isologia* within each city, that is, equal right to speak—*and isologia* in the representative assemblies of all the cities. And if you compare that to Rome, even to the popular assemblies in Rome, well there's just no comparison. You see that both in Demosthenes and in the *Oresteia* of Aeschylus: when the assembly opened up, the first thing that happened was that the herald said, 'Who wishes to speak?' And anybody could get the floor. That was *isēgoria*, equal right to address the *agora*.

"So I think that I add a useful component to this ongoing debate by calling attention to this very obscure bit of history, when the *graphē paranomōn* was used to defend the schools of philosophy. After all, Plato lived his whole life undisturbed, including forty years of teaching antidemocratic doctrine, and died in his bed. And this Demetrius of Phalerum, who was a real philosopher-king, was quite a jerk. He put statues of himself all over town. Very much corrupted by his power. After he was overthrown, he went to the great library in Alexandria and lived a useful life as a librarian.

"But you see, the first thing that the Macedonians did when they took over was to disenfranchise all the *poor* citizens—and, I think, most of the middle class, if not all. And the Romans did that, too. They would disenfranchise the poor and the middle class and leave the municipal power in the hands of the rich. And the rich preferred to submit to the great empires than to go on with democracy and the welfare state, both of which irked them."

RADICAL

"I've got about fifty volumes in xerox of rarities in classical studies. One reason I'm not at American University anymore is that my private library is better than theirs. I've got about a thousand volumes, as I'll show you tomorrow. Greek and Latin classics. It's all come out of my pocket. Since I was running a business, it was a business expense. Since I'm working on a project again, it's a business expense. I've never had a foundation grant in my life, I'm proud to say. They like innocuous scholarship, not the dangerous conclusions. There's something debilitating, though, about being a radical and being on the government's tit. Getting tax exemption to overthrow the government. Feuerbach, the German materialist philosopher, said, 'Ein mensch ist was er isst,' a man is what he eats. A radical should eat the bread of affliction. Not that I've been afflicted, I must say. I've been fortunate being able to make a living."

10

PM

We are against people who push other people
around, in this country or abroad. We propose
to crusade for those who seek constructively
to improve the way men live together.

Ralph Ingersoll
prospectus for *PM*, 1940

"RALPH INGERSOLL was wonderful. He'd been an engineer,
and he was a socialite. San Francisco has an upper crust, a
very nice upper crust. He was of it, but he broke away. One
thing he did that Stern didn't do was to break with conventions. Stern had a lot of experience as a reporter, and in all
of the other jobs. He came up from the ranks. Ralph came
in from the top, as it were. He broke up the stereotypes and
conventions of newspaper writing. He got us to write a news
story as a *story* and not to put in the guy's name and address
and his grandmother in the first paragraph. He'd have us
make the continuity and narration fit the circumstances of
the story. He really taught us a lot. *PM* was a different kind
of paper. It was a bit kooky. [Laughs.] Disorganized and all
of that, but it was a breath of fresh air in the American
newspaper business.

"I worked for him in the Washington bureau, and I just
worked my ass off. My biggest week I had a deadline Friday
morning for the *Nation*, and I wasn't able to get my work

done on Thursday. So I got an early morning plane, two o'clock or three o'clock, to New York, got in very early, had a steak at an all-night restaurant. Went in to the *Nation* office, wrote my weekly letter, about a page and a half, about 1,500 words. Wrote a long editorial and a paragraph before anybody came in. Went off to a Turkish bath, had a nap. Went over to *PM*, wrote a big story that made page one— you know, the cover. *PM* was in tabloid form. Then caught the *Congressional* back to Washington. It was a lot of work doing those two jobs. I got $150 from *PM* and $75 from the *Nation*. I just loved the guy the way I loved Stern. His book *The Battle Is the Pay-Off* is tremendous, beautifully written. Its depictions of men at war—it matches *The Red Badge of Courage*.

"I made friends at the San Francisco meeting [to found the United Nations] in 1945 with a number of Zionists who were there, and I was very drawn to the Zionist cause. I hadn't been a Zionist before the war in any strict sense. I did get *Young Judean* magazine in the twenties; I had read about kibbutzim. So that year I went to Palestine, got there the day the Haganah began the war with the British and blew up the watchtowers, the beginning of the illegal operation. And then in forty-six, a friend of mine from the Haganah took me out to Staten Island to see ships they were preparing for an illegal Navy for the Haganah to take refugees. He said would I like to go and, boy, I just was ready to go immediately. They said, 'We'll let you know. We don't want anyone to know about it.' There were some British correspondents at the *Nation*, so they didn't want the *Nation* to know about it. When I got word, I told Ralph Ingersoll. He and Esther were the only people I told. I was away on this illegal trip for a couple of months. I told my children that it was dangerous and that I might get shot. It was very nice of Esther to let me go. I was dying to go, just dying to go. When I got back, the *Nation* was mad at me. I realized that they would fire me, so I graciously resigned.

"At that time, there was a revolt in *PM*'s Washington bureau. Ken Crawford and Jimmy Wechsler were smearing Ralph as a party-liner, and he fired them and asked me to become head of the bureau. The only time I've ever been an executive. I really hated it. I hated having to fire people. Just awful. I had to fire some people at the *Weekly*, and I hated that.

"I really liked Marshall Field an awful lot, he was very good to me. And I realize that it was very hard for a man of his high social position in Chicago, with all that wealth, to support a bunch of nondescript radicals and pinkos in New York City. And I could just imagine him going to his clubs . . . It would be hard to take. At one point, I thought he was going to fire me. I was doing very tough coverage of the War Production Board, and I was criticizing Donald Nelson, a good friend of Marshall Field's. And word came that Field wanted to see me about a story I'd written. I was told to fly out to Chicago to see him. He was so nice, and he just said, 'How did you get that story?' And I told him, and he thought that was wonderful. He didn't scold me. He just wanted to talk. He was very shy. He would come into the office and say, 'Could I please have a copy of today's paper?' Very gentlemanly. It was wonderful of him to back up the paper.

"He put in something like a million and a half or two million dollars so the paper could have broken even at five cents in those days. The other papers were two cents. We were smaller. We could have broken even at 250,000 circulation. The only time we did that was with my *Underground to Palestine* series. We never had any advertising, that was Ingersoll's policy. We were caught in a bind.

"John P. Lewis, our managing editor, I loved very much. We got him when Ralph went off to war. He was a real old-fashioned nonintellectual newspaperman from Buffalo. It was amazing how he rode herd on a bunch of prima-donna New York Jewish and gentile intellectuals. He would give you confidence. He would say, 'You can do it, Izzy, don't be afraid.' And you'd feel like you could do it. He was a very good Toscanini for the orchestra. When he left, Joe Barnes from the *Herald Tribune* became the editor.

"We were trying to be a complete paper, and we didn't have the resources. It was nonsense. I was arguing that we ought to face up to it—we were a secondary paper. We should focus on exclusives and not do little feeble rewrites of stuff in the *Times*. Focus on two or three good stories. Scream it, and sell; provide some literary services. Ralph had pioneered many kinds of special coverage. But we just didn't have the numbers or the money. Ralph sold the paper in 1948 to Bart Crum of San Francisco. I had known him through some Communist connections. He had taken a part in the fight for a Jewish homeland. He changed the paper to the New York *Star*.

"I worked for the *Star*, and I had a lot of fun. Then, after a couple of years, Joe Barnes called me on a Friday night and said the paper was closing down. And I said to Esther, 'Now I'll really get a chance to write that book.' I don't know what book it was. But I didn't feel downhearted. I went upstairs to get a bath and there was a call from Ted Thackrey, who was now running the editorial page for Dolly Schiff at the *Post*, and he said, how'd I like to bring my column—on a daily basis—to the *Post*. I think I was writing a column three times a week at the *Star*. And he said, 'I'll pay you what they paid you.' So Albert Deutsch and I went to the *Post*, and it was wonderful. I didn't lose a day's work. I started on Monday at a good salary—I think I was getting $225 or $250 a week. He had to pay me twice as much as for three columns. So I worked for him, and I didn't get paid for a couple of weeks. It turns out, he had improvised this hiring without talking to Dolly. Pretty soon, though, he broke with her and bought the old *PM*-New York *Star*, renamed it the *Daily Compass,* and Deutsch and I went with him. Albert Deutsch was a very good writer on social questions. He had a social welfare and social justice column. He pioneered that kind of reporting.

"Ted Thackrey carried a very heavy burden. He was bankrolled by a Chicago lady, Anita McCormick Blaine, who was an heiress to the Harvester fortune. She ultimately put half a million dollars into it, but that's still chicken feed for a New York paper. Ted worked very hard to keep it alive. He was a gallant fellow. And he failed. It was a hopeless task. And the Friday before the election in November of fifty-two, he called up and said the paper was closing down.

"I thought I'd go back to the *Nation*. And I called Freda and asked her if I could get my job back as Washington editor—they had never found anyone to replace me. They really haven't found anybody to do the job I did. Because they really never got an all-around newspaperman. Before me, I had some good predecessors: Paul Anderson and Paul

Ward were both all-around newspapermen and did a good job. The people that followed were really not reporters in that way. Freda couldn't make up her mind. She was strapped financially—so I couldn't get her to say yes, and I couldn't get her to say no.

"I didn't get any severance pay out of the *Star*, so when Albert and I went up to the *Post* with Ted, we asked him to put up severance pay in escrow. So when the *Compass* closed down, I had severance pay of $3,500.

"I had thought of starting a paper, and I thought of cutting the cloth of the product to the actual size of the market. But there wasn't a big enough market, despite liberal talk, to support a liberal daily. So I thought, why not try a newsletter, a four-page newsletter. I raised the money from some other people. I was the biggest investor, at $3,500, one man put up $2,500, I had two interest-free loans and the others were small investors who just gave me the money. I paid it all back. I had subscription lists of the *Star* and the *Compass*, some *PM* readers, the teachers' union gave me their list. I had a list of people who had bought my *Hidden History of the Korean War* from Monthly Review. I had some very good lists. One list I got forty-five percent response from, and overall I got about a seven-and-a-half-percent response. That's a very good response in mail order. In those days, two and a half percent was thought to be good.

"I got 5,300 subscribers at $5 a piece, and by budgeting $500 a week out of that, I was able to cover my printing costs and a salary of $125 for myself and $75 for a girl in the office, whom I soon had to fire because she made me feel unwelcome in my own office, and Esther took over. We broke even.

"About two months before the end of the year, I got very nervous about renewals. I started out to raise some money, and I called a left-wing sympathizer in New York who shall remain nameless—he had made a lot of money in business. I said, 'Look, I need some money.' I said it right over the phone so he'd know I wasn't making a social call. And he said, 'Come on up.' So I went up to New York and had lunch with him. And he gives me a hundred-dollar bill. Jesus Christ, it cost me more than that to go up there. Renewals started trickling in so I decided that I'd give up trying to raise money. It's a pain in the ass. Some rich people are really nice, and I had a few people who were very nice. But others want to be wooed and wooed and wooed and made much of as they trickle you bits of jack—and the renewals were enough to carry me. And from that point on, through the growth of the paper and a very high renewal rate and a very good means of promotion, the paper grew to about 73,000 when I quit. I would always put in the paper, 'If you like an article, send me a stamped, self-addressed envelope, and I'll send a free copy to a friend.' Those were real prospects. Finally, the paper got off the ground very nicely, and I have a pension fund. I thought originally the paper might last just a couple of years, but I was determined to keep on doing what I wanted to do. I could have gotten a conventional job, I wasn't blacklisted. Some papers might have hesitated to hire me as a pinko, but I would have gotten a job. I'm a good newspaperman. I just wanted to do my stuff."

11

ADVERTISING

I. F. Stone's Weekly
March 21, 1953

"YEAH, I RAN AN AD ONCE. I'll tell you why. When I started
out I didn't have a Congressional press pass—I'd had them
at *PM*. When I inquired, they told me that you had to have
advertising. So, there was a man in New York named
Brooks—not Brooks Brothers!—and he gave me a suit in
exchange for an ad. It was a nice suit and, of course, I had
so many readers in New York. It was a fair exchange. Well,

then they told me that you had to have a *substantial* portion of your revenue from advertising. I just wasn't interested in that, in all that would have entailed as time went on. It just wasn't worth it. So I never got the press pass, but they gave me what they called the 'courtesy of the gallery.' I could go by anytime, except when the president was there. I guess they thought I was a threat! [Laughs.]"

12

THE ROSENBERGS/HISS

Who was telling the truth—the Rosenbergs or
Greenglass? Who was telling the truth—Sobell or
Elitcher? It will be a long time, if ever, before we
know for certain. We may wake up one morning
to learn that the Rosenbergs were guilty. We may
wake up to learn that they were innocent. But
I doubt whether we will ever find there was a
deliberate frame-up. Fanaticism had the same
momentum on both sides.

I. F. Stone's Weekly
July 2, 1956

"I NEVER READ the [Allen] Weinstein book [*Perjury: The Hiss-
Chambers Case*, 1978], but [Ronald] Radosh went back to a
piece I wrote in the *Weekly* a few years after the [Rosenbergs']
execution, and it's a pretty good piece, it stands up. Ted
Thackrey and I divided the work on the final appeals: he
read the evidence and I read the legal papers. By then it was
very voluminous, because there was both the Circuit Court
and the petition to the Supreme Court. And neither of us
felt that it was a simple frame-up or a simple civil-liberties
case. We didn't feel that they had a full and fair trial. We
thought the penalty was way out of line, but we didn't
think—we weren't sure—that they were guilty. But we didn't
think they were—well, we weren't very convinced they were

innocent, either. There was a lot of specious reasoning going on, on both sides. There was no 'secret' of the bomb once it was exploded, and the 'secret,' therefore, couldn't be transmitted, didn't have to be transmitted. On the other hand, you couldn't honestly argue that the Soviets might not benefit by having access to certain technological secrets. Not *the big* secret, but something that would help them to speed up their own acquisition. Obviously, both sides use espionage, and there *were* a lot of little secrets to be stolen. So the argument about the stuff that was given in the Rosenberg case—it may not have been terribly important, but it had some value.

"Great Britain handled the Fuchs affair much better. Fuchs was far more important and they gave him a ten-year sentence. And he left for East Germany. So . . . an agonizing experience. I didn't go to the big meeting in New York [a forum on the Rosenberg case, held at Town Hall, October 20, 1983], because I hated to see the Left tear itself apart over an issue where we've never been able to get to anything definitive. I think Radosh brought up some big and good things on both sides. I think the outrage at him was unjustified.

"On the Weinstein book, I felt that the *New York Review of Books* was very unfair. A *Herald Tribune* man [John Chabot Smith] had just published his own book on the Hiss case [*Alger Hiss: The True Story*, 1976] and before that book had a chance to be evaluated, even read, it was really destroyed by the Weinstein *review*! Weinstein claimed to be a liberal, but he ended up way over on the Right and in a plush job at Georgetown. I thought that was unfair. He had his book coming out and he was given a chance to destroy the other book. I didn't want to be a kind of dummy director, I hadn't been consulted on it, and I didn't want to bear responsibility on what I hadn't been consulted on, so I left the *New York Review*. The book by the *Herald Tribune* correspondent who covered the trial was just destroyed. And you know all of the right wing went to the *New York Review of Books*—for once!—as the gospel, the Bible, on this. I thought that it would have been more fair to let a more objective observer do it.

"I was never able to make up my mind about Hiss. I admired him when he and two others walked out of the Agriculture Department. There were two Section 7's in the New Deal that were controversial and crucial. There was the one that was in the National Recovery Act, giving labor the right to organize—although it had a lot of ambiguity in it. And there was the other, in the Triple A Act, designed to make sure that when the government subsidized a withdrawal of acreage from crops such as cotton, that part of the benefits would go to the sharecroppers and tenant farmers, so the big landowners couldn't take the money and keep it and throw the 'croppers and tenants off of the land. It was a very fundamental issue. Henry Wallace was then Secretary of Agriculture, and he wasn't what he became later on. He represented the big farmers. And Lee Pressman, Gardner Jackson, and Hiss walked out in protest. The New Deal tried to remedy a little of that, but it was never really enforced . . . So I admired Hiss for that. And I encountered him again when, as an editorial writer, I was covering the Nye investigation. Later on, he seemed like such a climber and a snob. Sucking up to John Foster Dulles.

"It's hard to believe, but there in Chambers's book [*Witness*, 1952], which always struck me as rather chrome-plated Dostoevesky, there were things that had a lot of verisimilitude in his picture of life inside the Party. But there were also things that I just didn't believe. The idea that he would be both a collector of dues and a Soviet agent at the same time seemed to me absolutely absurd. You see there were people like Victor Perlo who had been in the federal government and been purged—and Perlo, for example, ended up on the *Daily Worker*. Now he would have been a sitting duck if he was passing any secrets. But the government never laid a finger on him.

"When the attack on the Communists began in the spring of 1948, it was a way to scare liberals away from the Wallace campaign. The version that spread then was that the government was going to prove that the Party was a tremendous espionage agency. But the best that the government could do was a conspiracy indictment. And an indictment for conspiracy not to *overthrow* the government, but purely to *advocate*—that means, at some future time. This amounted to a confession that, really, the government, with all the informers they had in the Party, just didn't have a case.

"I thought Hiss's book [*In the Court of Public Opinion,* 1957] was not much of a book. I talked to Alger when he came out of jail and I really admired him for his composure and his—there's a whole spectrum of possibilities, and a lot of gray areas in that case. I do think he really had a case for a new trial. New trials, in American law, are not easily granted. Otherwise you disrupt the whole judicial process—everybody would be getting a new trial. There has to be substantial new evidence to warrant that.

"The Rosenberg case was opened up by William Rubin in the *Guardian*. The *Daily Worker* didn't get into the case until later. The *Guardian* could be described as fellow traveler, but it wasn't under Communist control. They dashed in where the Communists feared to tread and made a *cause célèbre* out of it and the whole world took it up. And the American Communists had to take it up, too. They were leery of it. I think they were leery because they wanted to keep their party clear of Soviet espionage. I read the appellate briefs at the time and I knew the lawyer for the Rosenbergs [Emanuel Bloch], and he was a very hard-working and admirable man. He had to operate under terrible difficulties. Well, he tried to argue it as a civil liberties case, and it was an espionage case. It had to be argued in terms of the evidence under the statute. Now the Espionage Act had been used in the First World War in an anti–civil-liberties way, because there was a provision against advocacy against the draft. That's how they got Eugene Debs. But the other parts of it *were* on espionage, a criminal act. So when they argued it as civil liberties it was almost like a confession that they didn't really have a very good case on the other stuff.

"It was really painful. I didn't go to that meeting because I thought it was all a lot of—all these lefties reliving the past. There was a wonderful story about it in the *Village Voice* by a man named Hoberman. It was marvelous, like a Kafka affair. And he uncovered, that underneath was a cult of the Rosenbergs as heroes who were trying to help the Soviet Union. So on the one hand, they were arguing that they were supposed to be innocent . . . Well, it all plays into the hands of reaction."

13

FRENCH

WHILE DISCUSSING MISTAKES in translations, I related to Stone the story of how the poet Delmore Schwartz was commissioned to translate Rimbaud's *A Season in Hell*. The only problem was that Schwartz really did not know French and attempted the project without a dictionary. His most egregious error was his translation of "*Je rêve, je rêve*," as "I review, I review."

"Sloppy mistake. I've come across *rêve* as a verb recently. Oh, I'll tell you where there's *rêve*, in Verlaine's 'Clair de lune.' Do you know that poem? Well, there's a line there . . . let me see if I can get it:

> *Votre âme est un paysage choisi*
> *Que vont charmant masques et bergamasques*
> *Jouant du luth et dansant et quasi*
> *Tristes sous leurs déguisements fantasques*
>
> *Tout en chantant sur le mode mineur*
> *L'amour vainquer et la vie opportune,*
> *Ils n'ont pas l'air de croire a leur bonheur*
> *Et leur chanson se mêle au clair de lune,*
>
> *Au calme clair de lune triste et beau,*
> *Qui fait rêver les oiseaux dans les arbres*

Rêver! 'That makes the birds dream, the birds dream in the trees' . . .

Et sangloter d'extase les jets d'eau,
Les grands jets d'eau sveltes parmi les marbres.

That's a wonderful poem!

Au calme clair de lune triste et beau,
Qui fait rêver les oiseaux dans les arbres . . .

Yeah. That's beautiful."

14

PLATO

George Anastaplo and I have in common, among other things, an admiration for Greek classics. The beginning of our differences, on the other hand, may be in the fact that I think most often of Fifth Century Athens and he thinks first of the Fourth Century great, particularly Plato and Aristotle. In the Fifth Century there was an accumulation of ideas from earlier Greek centers, particularly from Greek settlements in Italy and Asia Minor with its islands. Athens was the proud but disputed leader of the Greek world. In the Fourth Century she had lost her power; though in the end she defied Philip of Macedon. Plato emphasizes the failings of Athens, and he speaks of "Eastern" mysteries, while his extraordinary genius expressed many of the influences of the pioneer Fifth Century, with its buildings and sculptures, its comedies, trage-dies, great Sophists, and its historians. The funeral oration of Pericles presents an ideal of what Plato found a failure.

Malcolm P. Sharp
reviewing George Anastaplo's *Human Being and Citizen*
University of Chicago Law Alumni Journal,
Fall, 1976

IN HIS UNPUBLISHED LECTURES, Stone observes that there are two ways of fulfilling one's life. One is to be active, involved in society. The other is that favored by monastic orders and some Eastern traditions—to withdraw from the world to a life of contemplation. Stone feels that Socrates speaks for the second style, and does so in the face of the exemplary city of the first style. I asked Stone, however, if there were not more than just these two styles. Isn't Socrates' life a fulfilled life in the active sense, since he did live and participate in the city, even if he spoke against it? After all, he still lives now, in the debates of men throughout the world, some twenty-three hundred years later.

"Yeah, his life is fulfilled, but Plato fulfilled it for him. If we only had the Xenophonic Socrates, he wouldn't be the same figure. He's too banal. See, he says—he *keeps* saying—'we have to take care of our souls.' And the way you take care of your soul is like a medieval monk. You *withdraw* from the dirt of politics and purify your soul. Well now, the *polis*—it wasn't a matter of being active politically—the *polis* is a place where men *live together* in a community. And because they're part of a community, each man can do a different part and fulfill himself in any way he likes. If he's a speaker, he has an audience. If he's a poet, he has people ready to listen. If he's a philosopher, he has pupils. If he's a shoemaker, he has people who need shoes. If he's a political leader by instinct, he has a chance to show his stuff. A man on a desert isle with the same gifts would be barren. But living in a *polis* he takes part in a community. So, for the average man, for most people, the city was a way to fulfill yourself. Pericles, in the Funeral Speech in Thucydides, says that if anybody wants to be an *idiotēs*, which means a private citizen, he is rather looked down upon, as *apragmona*, but he can do it if he wants to. Plato, meanwhile, is always sneering at *polypragmosynēs*, that is, versatility. And the Athenians loved to think of themselves as versatile. And they were. But Socrates always preached 'each man to his last.' Well, if a shoemaker can only be a shoemaker, then he has a pretty narrow, restricted life. If he can also go to the theater, and listen to debates in the Assembly, and occasionally speak, or take part in a jury trial and assess questions of justice, he's educated. It's education. And what's so disappointing in Plato and Aristotle—in their rather snobbish vein—is that they don't recognize that the *polis*, especially Athens, was a great educational institution of lifelong learning, in which people, by participating, developed themselves. So I'm reacting to that. Socrates had a chance to fulfill himself in *his* own way— and I see no reason why he should not have had it. The city depends on variety, and he provided an interesting variety.

"But he's held up as somebody who was in touch with other forces—as the voice of the *daimonion*. So he's a sacred figure. But teachers don't call attention to the other sides of the question. Actually, he lived for seventy years and was undisturbed. He was a town character, lovingly described in the *Clouds*, and elsewhere. Pretty well ticked off in the *Birds* and in the *Frogs*. But then, after the terrible events of 411, 404, and 401 [B.C.], there he was, back at the game of teaching these young rich snobs to sneer at the city. The same crowd of people that ran the tyranny of the Thirty—Charmides and Critias—appear in the dialogues as very honored figures.

"You beg the question of justice in the *Republic*. I went to the Supreme Court yesterday to hear my brother-in-law [Leonard Boudin] argue a freedom-of-travel case [*Regan* v. *Wald*, the Reagan administration's case against free travel by Americans to Cuba]. Before the court got to it, they handed down some decisions on disputes among corporate interests. See, Plato got *rid* of the whole problem of social justice between classes, which can be absolute or can be relative. For example, when we had workmen's compensation laws, that was a case of proving class justice. It didn't treat the working class as equal to the rich, but it gave them some benefits. The problem of class justice covers a wide strata. Plato wipes all of that out by assuming a perfect government and a perfectly submissive lower class who are excluded from speech or participation or political power. Very much like Sparta, where the tillers of the soil were serfs. And the craftsmen—the *perioikoi*, 'those who live around us'—they were like the metics in Athens. They never got citizenship. The only full citizens even in Sparta were those who could afford to make the contribution to the upkeep of the common meals. Those who became poor and couldn't afford to make the contribution were relegated to a second-class status in Sparta. In fact, the number of actual Spartans decreased terribly as the years went on.

"So all of this is wiped out. And then Plato ignores the problem that even if you settle class problems, there are always disputes within the ruling class itself. I mean, right before his eyes, there were philosophers who never agreed.

What he really assumes is that the city is going to be ruled by devout Platonists; but within a century of the death of Plato, the Academy itself was taken over by absolute skeptics. Absolute skeptics. And you might say that that was a natural outgrowth of his teachings."*

* The reader may discover some surprising similarities between Stone's observations on Socrates and those of the right-wing political scientist Willmoore Kendall in "The People versus Socrates Revisited," originally published in *Modern Age* (Winter 1958–59), and reprinted in *Willmoore Kendall: Contra Mundum* (1971). Readers interested in other independent viewpoints on Plato are referred to James Redfield's "A Lecture on Plato's *Apology*," *Journal of General Education* (July 1963); George Anastaplo's "Human Being and Citizen: A Beginning to the Study of Plato's *Apology of Socrates*," in *Human Being and Citizen* (1975); and David Grene, *Man in His Pride* (1950). Grene has observed that "we must try to avoid a falsity of emphasis such that . . . we are led to identify Plato superficially with modern political doctrines because specific parts of his total picture recall them." Some of the authors cited in this note may be what Stone calls "devout Platonists."

15

FREE SPEECH

As with many in the 1950s, Stone's advocacy of free speech for Communists often led to charges that Stone supported the aims of the Communist Party. While Stone was often in agreement with the Communists and other left-wing groups in their critique of American capitalism and social policy, he always distanced himself from the antidemocratic tendencies in these movements. Nevertheless, because of his advocacy of both free speech and social change during a time when both were seen as suspect, Stone's overriding concern with freedom of thought often appeared lost in the shuffle. I was concerned about articles that he had published in the early fifties that appeared to support the Supreme Court ruling in the 1951 *Dennis* case, which upheld the conviction of the first group of Communist Party leaders prosecuted under the Smith Act. Did Stone truly believe that a "clear and present danger" test was consonant with the protections of the First Amendment?

"No I don't accept that test, and I didn't. I was attacking the court for not applying its own standards. I didn't see any clear and present danger—neither would Jefferson—in an indictment for 'conspiracy to advocate.' It's pretty goddamned farfetched, and Jefferson would feel that way too. That test goes back to an opinion Holmes wrote in the *Schenck* case in 1919 [upholding the convictions of Socialist Party leaders for their opposition to the draft in the First

World War]. And I think he was wrong there, too. He used an oversimplified analogy. He said, 'Does a man have a right to cry "Fire!" in a crowded theater?' My answer to that would be that a man who cries 'Fire!' in a crowded theater—especially if he does it with malice and knowledge that it wasn't true—would be guilty of provoking a public disorder under circumstances that did lead, or might have led, to loss of life. So it could be punishable as a criminal act. By keeping such an act away from free speech, you keep your free speech principle pure. For example, if you get up and make a speech advocating the murder of blacks or Jews, that's advocating murder. It's incitement to crime, and incitement to crime is a crime in itself.

"There are always blurs on the edges of everything. And one of the problems of the law is to keep those edges as clear as possible and to use categories that can prevent the pollution of a fundamental liberty. For example, there is an anti-insurrection law that goes back to the Civil War, and they could have gone after the Communists under that. If you plan to seize power by seizing post offices, radio stations, things like that, that's insurrection, and it's not a matter of political freedom. Political freedom does not include the right to seize power, but in Jefferson's view, it does include the right to affirm revolutionary doctrines or doctrines that have revolutionary implications. Otherwise, they'd have turned their backs on their own actions, on the American Revolution, and restricted the area of proposals for social change. So I don't agree with the *Schenck* doctrine. I was just trying to show that even within the court's own context, the Communists had not committed any crime."

16

WONDERFUL TOWN

"THIS IS A WONDERFUL CAPITAL to cover things in because there's an awful lot of information available despite the growth of secrecy and so on. For example, when I had the *Weekly* and there would be an explosion in a country I didn't know a damn thing about, and I had to go to press in two days. I had to write an article for a weekly—that's a little more reflective than a daily story. You can have room to move and a little extra time to give it depth. So what do you do? If it's a country that depends on, say, copper, you go to the Bureau of Mines in the Interior Department and you get the latest report on copper. And the report on the copper industry will give you a sense of the basic social-economic factors that are working in that country, and you'll understand it better. If it's soybeans, you go to the Agriculture Department and get the latest few crop reports. I got a good hell of a news story before the Korean War when I discovered that the Kuomintang in China were buying soybean futures as if they knew something was coming, and then there was a Senate investigation, and they *did* know something.

"The Commerce Department has very good country studies for investors. And they're on a very high level of objectivity and factuality. You don't have to take their conclusions. Read them like a radical, with a sense of history and a sense of class forces. But you have the basic material there. If you know where to look, you can bone up on a good story within twenty-four hours, and cover the news, but cover it in perspective, so people know what makes it tick.

"Skip the State Department. I detest them. I didn't like them in the twenties . . . If you go to the cafeteria of each department, you see that they each have their own character, their own gestalt, or personality. If you go to Agriculture and you go to the State Department, you'll see two different Americas, and two kinds of Americans. The State Department is not dominated by the preppies the way it used to be, but the East Coast WASP preppie still sets the tone. Some guys come in from Missouri or California and they're all buttoned up, they act like they went to Exeter. The foreign services consider themselves an elite, and wherever they go they deal with the wealthy and the rich and the aristocracy, and they have cheap servants, and all of a sudden they get an inflated ego. They get used to being served, and they lose their democratic character. And they instinctively sympathize with undemocratic forces.

"Before the Second World War they were very unsympathetic to refugees from Italian fascism, from Nazism. They weren't fascists, just meanspirited bureaucrats. We had two good antifascist ambassadors, both historians. One was William E. Dodd, in Berlin, who wrote *Cotton Kingdom* on the Old South, and Claude Bowers, then in Madrid. And the State Department bureaucracy made life miserable for them. Just about every president has trouble with the State Department. Roosevelt did too. They weren't on the same wavelength as the New Deal.

"You get a lot of malarkey there, but you can learn things

even from malarkey. For example, when the State Department issued its famous White Paper on Vietnam. A good way to read a government document is backward. They're very long, and you get the clues in the last pages. For example, the *Federal Budget*—it's huge. You can get a double hernia carrying it back to your office. But the final supplement volume, called *Special Analyses and Topics*, that's where you often find the body buried. Or the statistics in the back. People tend to read instead the 'Message of the Secretary' or whoever's getting the thing out.

"Well, I got the White Paper on a Thursday and read it very carefully, including the figures on the infiltration of troops from North Vietnam. It was for release on Monday. I went over to the Pentagon. I must say, I like the Pentagon better than the State Department. All clichés have some value and some limitation—not everybody in the military service is a martinet, a pyromaniac and militaristic monster. And if a reporter goes over there on a story and has boned up first . . . You can't sit on their lap and ask them to feed you secrets—then they'll just give you a lot of crap. But if you're boned up in advance on a story and have good questions, they'll respect you for your professionalism. And many of them would rather tell the truth than lie. If you can ask questions that really pin them down you can learn quite a lot.

"Anyway, I began to get their figures on infiltration from the North. They were very different from the State Department's. And they didn't know that the State Department issued a White Paper with its own stuff. So I wrote a piece in which I used military figures to make a mockery of the State Department.

"The Vietnam War was one of the best-covered wars we ever fought. There was more truth about the Vietnam War in the papers than any war we were ever in—people just don't read papers carefully. One reason that it was so well covered was that when you got out there, you found American officers—military, AID, foreign service, intelligence—who were really pissed off with Washington. They *knew* what was going on, they were writing a lot of good reports, and very little was getting through to the capital. A bureaucracy is like a sieve, and as a report went from the field to Saigon, some of the tough stuff got taken out. And then to the command headquarters, where some more went, and by the time it got to Washington, it was full of crap. And they would spill the beans and talk their hearts out to reporters.

"And you have special investigations and hearings—for example, on Star Wars. Editors discourage young writers from going into this stuff. They say, 'It's all pig iron, it's all a bunch of goddamned pig iron. Give us something hot.' Well, right after the president's message on Star Wars, there was a one-day hearing on this cuckoo business. Very badly covered. Two subcommittees of the House heard from all sides on it. The best testimony came from the Pentagon, strangely enough. Richard Delauer, the undersecretary of defense in charge of research and development, gave a marvelous exposition. He didn't attack SDI. But he exposed it in a real sense. He showed how it involved action in about half a dozen different sets of atmospheric conditions, each of them so different that they involved technological problems as expensive and difficult to handle as the Apollo Project or the Manhattan Project. He showed how complicated it was. He subsequently retired.

"You can't be a prisoner of stereotypes. You can't be a know-it-all smart ass, starting out a story thinking you know all about it and you know what the guy is going to say and that he's just a brass hat or this or that. You can't be a prisoner of your preconceptions. Another example, then-General Charles Gabriel was head of the U.S. Air Force—he appeared at a hearing on antisatellite weapons that very few people covered or paid attention to. This was the first step toward weapons in space. The Russians had called for a moratorium. Now, in this hearing, Gabriel, in written answers to written interrogatories, as well as in response to oral questioning, gave very thoughtful testimony. He said that *we* had greater interest in a moratorium than the Russians for the simple reason that we had a technologically advanced society and that we were much more dependent, in our business and civil life, as well as in the military, on satellite communication. And it's very easy to blind them, to blow them out. And he was reprimanded for that testimony! I called the chairman of the committee and suggested that he recall General Gabriel and ask him if it was true that he got reprimanded for telling the truth under oath. It was a big story, and it got a paragraph in the major papers and Gabriel was just reduced to silence.

"But it's a wonderful capital to cover. If you started out covering small towns like I did in southern New Jersey, where it's hard as hell to find a story—you've got to think up things for the mayor to say, or a good sermon for the minister. A young Jewish atheist, I was the church editor for five dollars a sermon. The ministers were a nice bunch of guys, they liked me, and I liked them. I would suggest a topic and get a good story. But here, it's apple pie. You can be a sycophant. You can sit on your rear end in the Press Club and write from the press releases. You can be a pet and a sucker for the establishment. Or you can be a heretic and a maverick. You can do anything you damn please. It's a big place. It's still very open. You can make your own terms.

"But if you're assigned to a specific agency, you're up against a tough proposition, unless you've got a boss who will really back you up. Because if you're too independent, they can slip a scoop to your opposition. Or they can call up your boss and say, 'This young fellow you've got down here—he's not a Communist, we know he's not a Communist, we don't go in for that stuff anymore—but he certainly writes some very peculiar stories!' And, you know, your publisher is a guy who made five million dollars in the toilet paper business and thinks that made him a journalist and he doesn't know from nothing and he picks up his ideas in the locker room of a country club. And he wants to know if there isn't really a problem with your stuff.

"I remember in the early 1930s. The New York *Times* was *awful*. You look back in the files, you'll see what I'm talking about. Richard V. Oulihan was the chief Washington correspondent. He used to play medicine ball with Herbert Hoover every morning at the White House. That's enough to kill off a good reporter. Not because it was medicine ball. But you *cannot get intimate* with officials and maintain your independence. No matter whether they are good guys or bad guys. Don't get intimate with them or you lose your independence and they'll use you.

"But if you're just a one-man band covering the whole town, if you get low one place, the hell with it, you go to another. And the bureaucrats are scared. Even if you only have a fly sheet—they're scared of having it in print. The sources of information are tremendous. You have the authorization and appropriation hearings, special investigations, documents. You can get a lot of material that very few reporters have the time to read or care to read. The more these things say, the more they reveal. And even from within the bureaucracy itself, there are often honest men who speak out. And very often the press does a lousy job of covering it."

17

BIBLE

STONE IN HIS LECTURES points to the "democracy of the Bible." Does he find that the view in support of social justice and equality expressed in the Prophets and the New Testament Gospels is also found in the basic text of the Hebrew Bible—the Five Books of Moses, the Torah?

"Yes, I think it is. Because the idea that man was made in the image of God was a very democratic and elevating idea. That's right in the opening chapters of Genesis. And the fact that everybody has a common father and mother, that's democratic. I don't see any *anti*democratic teaching in Deuteronomy. And the Prophets, of course, go further in the search for social justice, away from the jealous, tribal God. And in the Gospels it's even *stronger*. The revolutionary proletarian thing is even stronger in the Gospels.

"You shouldn't be misled by references to kingship in the Bible. They didn't move into that for quite a while. There was a long period between the conquest of the Holy Land and the establishment of the two kingdoms. Kingship in the Bible was not what we think of as absolute kingship in the modern world. Kingship in ancient Greece was not what we think of as kingship in the modern world. Even in Homer—Agamemnon was not an absolute monarch.

He's *primus inter pares*. He's first among equals. And when the plague comes, he has to give up the slave girl that he grabbed. So you mustn't think of kingship in the Bible in the same way that you think of Louis XIV. And it wasn't a hierarchical society, in the way we speak of today."

18

THE SOPHISTS

IN HIS LECTURES, Stone says that the sophists have been unfairly maligned. I asked him what he meant by this.

"It was Grote, in his famous chapters on the history of Greece, who shed new light on this. I mean to treat all these teachers, these 'sophists,' as if they had a common doctrine and a common view and to take all this snobbish aristocratic shit out of Plato about not selling your learning. He was a rich man—he didn't *have* to sell his learning. And here are a lot of college professors who depend on their salaries—and there's nothing wrong with that—and they go ahead and accept all of this crap at face value. But ask *them* to serve without pay! It's nonsense. And it's vicious nonsense because it reflects a nineteenth-century world in which members of parliament in England and Germany were not paid a salary, so poor men couldn't afford to be elected, even if they *were* elected."

19

REAGAN

"You know, Lincoln, in the First Inaugural, talked about 'the better angels of our nature.' It's a wonderful phrase. Reagan has been appealing to the *worse* angels of our nature. There's a subliminal appeal: 'Get what you can.' 'It's my money, I don't want to pay taxes.' The gimme's. 'The hell with the future, the hell with the atmosphere.' It's really a very unpatriotic spirit Reagan has brought in. 'Enrich yourself.' 'The hell with the poor. The hell with your obligations.' He's not patriotic at all. The so-called yuppies are making money by the bushel. The middle class—this has always been a very middle-class country with a wide distribution of property, and that's made for great stability and for democracy. And the Reagan economic policies have destroyed parts of the middle class—the independent farmer, the organized worker in the smokestack industries. For the first time we're getting a real American proletariat—dishwashers, the guy who delivers pizza. He comes to town talking about balanced budgets! He's the biggest faking sonofabitch we've ever had in the capital. He's spent more money than all the other presidents up to this time. And most of it on this crazy arms race."

20

ECLC

"THE REASON I JOINED the Emergency Civil Liberties Committee [ECLC] was because the ACLU had fired two Communist directors, including Elizabeth Gurley Flynn. I felt very deeply that—well, I'll tell you a story. When I got back from Europe, this was in, I think, June of fifty-one, people were afraid to start organizations, because of the witch hunting. So they would have *ad hoc* groups to do certain things and then dissolve. So an *ad hoc* group from Syracuse, New York, called me up and said they were having a meeting to defend the Communists in the first Party case. Would I come and speak? I said yes, I would. So then they called me a couple of weeks later. They'd hired a big hall in Syracuse, but the American Legion was protesting the meeting. What should they do? I said, 'Invite the American Legion to send a representative and tell them that in the discussion period after the speech, I'll recognize him and give him a chance to speak.' So that's what happened, and I went up there, and after my speech the Legionnaire got up and said, 'Look, we agree with you about civil liberties and about freedom of speech and of the press. But we don't think that it ought to be given to people that don't believe in freedom of speech and of the press and who are against the very foundations of our society.'

"So I said, 'Well now, that's a view that's shared by many respected lawyers. And the most famous lawyer who's

113

argued that point of view is Andrei Vishinsky, Stalin's procurator general.' And I said, 'If you get his book *The Law of the Soviet State*, which is available in English,'—it had been published by Columbia University Press—'and you read his chapter on civil liberties, you'll see he takes the same position as the American Legion. Vishinsky says, Look, we've got a wonderful constitution, in some ways even better than the American one, because not only do we have freedom of the press, but freedom of *access* to the *materials* of the press. Anybody can come to the government and be allocated time at a press free of charge to express his views. It's even *better* than the American Constitution. But we're not going to give it to those that are against the foundations of our society.' I said, 'Once you establish that loophole in the Constitution, then the first thing that happens is that those who are *fundamentally* critics of the system are excluded, so you no longer have real debates. There are no *if*s and *but*s in the First Amendment. Or in Jefferson's views. Secondly, people that claim that they're not against the system but only against the *abuses* of the system may be people who secretly are against the system but don't want to say that for fear of being excluded. So, like ADAers, they say that they're anticommunist, but they're really anticapitalist. So the result is that you put a damper on constructive criticism as well as destructive criticism, and you end up where they ended up in the Soviet Union, with no freedom of speech or press, except for those who agree one hundred percent with the government.'

"Well, he had no answer to that. So I and a group including Jimmy Wechsler signed a statement—he was then an *ex*-Communist—and we defended Elizabeth Gurley Flynn, saying the supposed purge was a violation of her rights. And I later argued that if you weren't going to defend the rights of the Communists and Trotskyists, then you were making a fundamental breach of the First Amendment that would have great harm. And I joined in organizing the ECLC for that reason, along with Corliss Lamont and Paul Lehmann of the Princeton Theological Seminary. I'm still a director. Though where I really disagree with some of the people there is that I believe that it's one world and you can't be for civil liberties here and against civil liberties in the Soviet Union. And some of them really take that position—although they do take up Communist dissidents, Trotskyists and so on."

21

YIDDISH

"I GREW UP SPEAKING ENGLISH, but my mother was ill after I was born and my grandmother and grandfather took care of me when I started to talk, so my first language was Yiddish. My father bought a store out in Richmond, Indiana, a very small gentile town. I went out there at about three, and they tell me I went out in the street and started talking *mame-loshen* to the schoolchildren. By the time I got to kindergarten there, I was fluent in English. Yiddish is a very tender language.

"My parents were not religious. They didn't eat pork or ham, and we tried not to mix milk and meat too much. But actually, the dietary laws were not observed. I grew up in Haddonfield, an old Quaker WASP town. There was no *cheder*, just a couple of Jewish families. So we didn't belong to a synagogue, and I didn't go to a Jewish school. But my uncle taught me Hebrew for my *bar mitzvah*. That was bible Hebrew. I remember my father taking us to Philadelphia to see the Yiddish theater, and I saw some wonderful things at the Yiddish Art Theatre. I saw Romain Rolland's *Wolves*, done in Yiddish. I saw Sholem Asch's *Got fun nekome*, God of Vengeance. Have you ever seen that? It's a wonderful play about a Jewish brothel keeper who is careful about his own daughter, but she slips into the same thing.

"My parents were Democrats. There weren't many

Democrats in Haddonfield! [Laughs.] In 1916, when I was
in elementary school, the only other boy who was a Democrat was an Irish Catholic boy, the only Irish Catholic
boy in the class. So we were both Democrats and Wilson-
ians. The first election that I remember was 1916. I was
very much for Wilson, and we went to bed thinking that
he had lost, and in the morning my father was shouting
upstairs that California had come through and that Wilson
had been elected. The only political act by my father I
remember was that when the armistice was declared to the
First World War—our store was right across the street from
the tallest building in town, the bell tower of the local fire
department, and my father wanted to ring the bell. He was
told that that would be a false alarm, and he'd be fined five
dollars. So he paid the five dollars and rang the bell! [Laughs.]

"You could always tell the politics of a Jewish household
in those days by which Jewish paper they subscribed to.
If they were Communists they got the *Freiheit*; if they were
socialists they got the *Forvits*, the *Forward*; if they were
religious they got the *Morning Journal*; if they were liberal,
they got the *Tug*, the *Day*. We took the *Tug*. From a
literary point of view, it was the best, the most literate of
the papers. I remember reading about Chinese philosophy
and things like that.

"My *machetonim*, the parents of my son-in-law—his
mother was the daughter of an anarchist who started a
community up in north Jersey. And that's where Will Durant was, too. A very idealistic community. I guess they
were Kropotkin-followers. I didn't have that type of influence on me. My introduction to radicalism and to socialism was through books. There was a big market in

popular editions of radical writers before the First World War. And after. I remember reading Franz Oppenheimer's *The State*. The one I remember the most was Kropotkin. A communism without coercion, without cops. Seemed ideal. When I first went to Palestine in forty-five and encountered the *Hashomer Hatza'ir* kibbutzim, it seemed to me Kropotkin's ideal. You know, nobody got stuck as a bureaucrat in those colonies. All the offices were rotated. Bureaucracy couldn't build up, and humble tasks and elevated tasks were all shared."

22

BLACKLIST

HUAC reads him and it cites him,
Alsop reads him and indicts him,
Reston reads him and rewrites him,
But the Stone goes rolling on!

"The Stone Goes Rolling On,"
E. Y. (Yip) Harburg,
on the occasion of Stone's 60th birthday
and the *Weekly*'s 15th anniversary

ONE QUESTION that ran through my mind as I researched Stone's background and publications was why he was not, as a self-proclaimed radical in the 1950s, called before any of the various investigative committees or subjected to any other government harassment.

"I've been asked that question and I don't know what the answer is. I used to say, when people asked me that years ago, I said, 'I don't know, but look—like Gypsy Rose Lee, I was taking it off every week, there was nothing left to expose.' And suppose they had brought me up there. So what. I mean, everybody assumed I was Karl Marx's baby brother, in the oversimplified atmosphere of Washington. And they were looking for big game. They were looking for guys on big papers that would really be a sensation. It wouldn't be much of a sensation to prove I was a Marxist-

Leninist. I had a small circulation and I wasn't hiding my views.

"I remember one day at a hearing of the McCarthy Committee I saw Roy Cohn pointing me out to Joe McCarthy. And I remember, somewhat wryly, how after McCarthy's downfall I was waiting for a taxi outside the Senate Office Building, trying to get a cab in the dusk. And who should come across the street from the direction of the Capitol but Joe McCarthy, looking very downcast and disreputable. You know the passage of the censure resolution really broke his will—and it broke his heart. It was a wonderful way to deal with him. He wasn't sent to jail. He wasn't thrown out of the Senate. He was just censured as a no good sonofabitch by his 'peers.' And he looked at me and said hello and I snubbed him. And I thought, why did I have to snub him?

"He was such a phony sonofabitch. He didn't even really believe in anticommunism. I once saw him get into an elevator with Acheson, and he was so affable: 'Hi Dean! Hi Dean!' You know, the other guy, McCarran, was a Catholic fascist. But McCarthy—this guy had been with the Communists and had shifted—he was really an adventurer.

"And it's interesting that I got my second-class mail privilege without any trouble. I appreciate it. And when I went abroad in fifty-six, I had to apply for a passport, and I had to sign a noncommunist oath. I hated like hell to do it. I was really getting claustrophobic. In a way, I think it was a violation of principle to sign it, but I did. Yeah, I did. They could have tried to get me for perjury. But by fifty-six, McCarthy was already in decline. You see, the witch hunt was very hit-or-miss, too. The ex-Communists who went into Wall Street, for example, and there were a number of them, were left alone. It was a kind of gilded Sahara. There were good friends of mine who either were Communists or were fired from the government as Communists. Some of them became millionaires and helped to finance the McGovern campaign, and remained good people. Some ex-Communists were so brokenhearted by the Khrushchev speech, they were like Catholics. I mean, if there's no Virgin Birth then they just washed their hands of the whole thing. You know what I mean? So, I don't know why, but that's about it."

I had asked Stone this question bearing in mind, of course, the *de facto* blacklist that had limited his opportunities for publication during the fifties. Every newspaper that he had worked for in this period had closed, in large part because of the political climate; and Freda Kirchwey had, for whatever reasons, balked at taking Stone back at the *Nation* after Ted Thackrey's *Daily Compass* folded. Stone was writing in a time of a general political paralysis.

"It was like decimation. You know, 'decimation' means killing one out of every ten men in an army to intimidate the army. And it poisoned the whole atmosphere and it frightened a lot of people. And destroyed a lot of careers. It was more moderate than Soviet witch hunts, certainly. They weren't destroyed in the way dissidents were in Russia."

In 1941, Stone was banished from the National Press Club. His crime? Bringing a black judge to the club as his lunch guest. Stone applied for readmission in 1956.

"You needed twenty-five cosponsors to support your application. I got nine. Nine! They let me back in in 1981, forty years after they put me out. The town was filled with such cowards then . . . "

23

SECRETS

"PEOPLE SAY—it's the conventional wisdom—that we can't do anything about Russia, we can't change Russia. There's a lot of truth in that. But it's not the whole truth. It's very hard for us to change Russia for the better. It's very easy for us to change Russia for the worse. What we do with our relations affects *us* immediately as well, because of the two superpowers' ability to destroy each other on the planet. J. Robert Oppenheimer called them two scorpions in a bottle. It's a marriage of hate, and each side poisons the other. If we don't come to an arms agreement and stop this crazy arms race, the Russians will tighten up at home, and we will here. We've had epidemics of anticommunist paranoia and hysteria now many times in my lifetime in which everything America is supposed to stand for was trampled on—the right to travel, the right to speak . . . The atmosphere will be worse.

"But more importantly, if we go into space war, we go into a type of weaponry that, in terrestrial terms, is almost instantaneous. The question is not, Can there be an umbrella? There can't be an umbrella. The question is speed. There won't be time to obey the Constitution and call in Congress and get a declaration of war. There won't be time to get the president out of bed! Those guys in the Politburo won't know what's going on. It means the end of political life.

"In such a situation, military secrets take on a new meaning, a new intensity. The fear of a strike, or a preemptive strike, it's going to increase tension to an unbearable degree. Under those circumstances, civil liberties are going to be in grave danger in our own country, as well as in Russia. In this sense, we have as deep a stake as the Russians in bringing this thing to a halt. So if *glasnost* fails in Russia, there will be less *glasnost* here, more secrecy here.

"This whole business of intelligence, it's a waste of money, highly overrated. You don't understand what's happening in history or in your time by peeking through keyholes. Look at this Iran business, it's ridiculous. With all the goddamned intelligence men we have in this city, to have a half-assed president talking about giving arms to Iran because it's on the Persian Gulf. Great discovery! It's on the Persian Gulf! When everybody in the Middle East, and elsewhere, who's thoughtful knows that Khomeini represents the most revolutionary, destabilizing force in the world today. If he breaks through on Iraq—I don't like the Iraq dictatorship—but if he breaks through there, it's going to destroy the whole Middle East. He's a Mohammedan Cromwell, a puritan fanatic with a great underground appeal in all the Arab countries. He'll upset the Mubarak regime in Egypt. We'll be at war very easily with Iran through some mishap in the Gulf to defend Saudi Arabian oil reserves. We look like stupid stumblebums.

"What's the good of all the money we spend on intelligence? When they get an intelligence report that has something in it, they ignore it. They don't like to read. They want everything on one piece of paper.

"When you get a report—I've never read a classified

intelligence report. I've never had access to that kind of poop. Fortunately. But Rand Corporation reports are very much like them. I've read quite a few of those. What are they? At their best, they're damn good magazine articles. Worth reading and considering, but when it comes to your desk, stamped 'Secret' or 'Top Secret' or 'Eyes Only,' it becomes sort of sacred poop. It's the hot stuff. It's inside stuff, and nobody challenges it. It may be full of errors. And the errors become government policy. There are very few things that are really secret or remain secret for very long. Basically, an intelligence service is there to tell the boss he's doing the right thing. It's very overrated and we're swamped with these organizations.

"We're becoming a partially closed society. It's a terrible concept. There's a whole string of Americans who have access to secret information, some of which is quite wrong and quite false. And debates go on behind closed doors and policy is made. And those few members of Congress who have access to the oversight committees become prisoners of the intelligence apparatus because they can't say what they've seen. And if they come out and criticize, they can't produce the proof, because the proof is classified. It's a disease. When I was in Russia, the phone book was classified. The dictators in the Politburo, they don't know what's going on. You don't know what's going on if you depend on cops, on secret police. Paranoia is a disease of secret police. They're paid to be suspicious of their grandmothers. And that isn't the way you understand people or what is going on. We're getting Sovietized in this country. Thank God it's nowhere near as bad, but it's creeping."

24

FILM STAR

According to the Parisian *L'Aurore*, I. F. Stone is the great star of the Cannes Film Festival.

Vincent Canby
New York *Times*
May 23, 1974

IN THE FALL OF 1973, nearly two years after the closing of the *Weekly*, filmmaker Jerry Bruck, Jr., released his hour-long black-and-white documentary, *I. F. Stone's Weekly*. Some three years in the making, the film, narrated by New York *Times* columnist Tom Wicker, was a critical smash and even something of a commercial success. The film follows Stone on his daily rounds during the final year of the *Weekly*, and includes footage of Stone's interviews and speaking engagements, as well as meetings with old friends such as the late Ralph Ingersoll, Stone's publisher at *PM*. The film introduces its viewers to what Peter Osnos, who was Stone's assistant for ten months in 1965 and 1966, and is now associate publisher of Random House, called "the classic view" of Stone's news gathering: "picking up a newspaper, which he grabs at midseam, and sort of tears in two." Bruck's film also brings to the screen Stone's famous basement files; the brimming newsstand of Dickie Nash, whom Stone calls "my only friend in downtown Washington during the Cold War"; and Jim Eudy and Carl McDonald, the Maryland printers who printed the *Weekly* for eighteen years. While the scene of Stone dropping the folded papers into his corner mailbox is a tender portrait of his entrepreneurship, the tearful farewell between Stone and his printers is a poignant reminder to Stone's subscribers that the *Weekly* is no more.

"The film was wonderful. I don't say that out of ego. I normally don't pay attention to stuff about me. It's boring to read about yourself. But the movie caught quite a lot. He used the juxtaposition of my stuff in the *Weekly* with documentary excerpts of all the big-boy Washington quack-quacks to real effect. My wife and I went to Cannes for the critic's week when Jerry's film played. I love movies, so it was great fun. I told the [New York] *Times* man that with all these experimental films, somebody ought to make one where boy meets girl, boy kisses girl, and then . . . the camera just cuts away. I'd like to see that. It'd be revolutionary!"

PERICLES

"A friend asked me how it was going with my Greek. I said, 'I do all right.' He said, 'Can you really understand it?' I said, 'I do my best. I get by.' 'Well Izzy,' he said, 'if Pericles came back, could you talk with him?' I said, 'Sure. If he spoke Yiddish.' "

25

"LITERATURE"

Academic disputation today has been aptly charac-
terized by a prominent scholar who remarked that
the proper way to refute someone is to ignore him.

Harry V. Jaffa

ONE CAN SEARCH IN VAIN through much of the literature of
the periods in which Stone was active as a journalist for as
much as a mention of his name. While I combed through
dozens of indexes, "Stimson, Henry L." and "Stone, Harlan
F." began to seem like old friends. There are a number of
reasons for Stone's absence from standard works. He was
not of the establishment, and he was not of the "establishment" anti-establishment. He was not a New Yorker, and
he was not in *The New Yorker*. Because of the solitariness of
his publication, he remained outside the general journalistic
fraternity. And because of his suspicion and distrust of conventional two-party politics, he remained outside of the general liberal framework. He was, despite his writing contemporary history that was well-documented and that has for
the most part stood the test of time, without academic credentials or affiliations. He was, because of his advocacy of
unpopular causes and his lack of concern with prestige, often
beyond the pale of respectable discourse.

All of these are parts of an explanation for Stone's continued position as an outsider. But, taken separately, they seem more like excuses than reasons. Because it is Stone's exclusion by writers on the left that is most distressing. Stone is absent from the references of the Cold War "revisionist" historians, just as he is from almost all the surveys of the intellectual and cultural climate of the postwar period. While his quasi–blacklist status might have had something to do with his omission from works in the forties and fifties, today's critics and historians perpetuate the offense. Richard H. Pells, in his thoughtful survey of the postwar intellectual scene in America, *The Liberal Mind in a Conservative Age*, gives Stone three walk-on appearances, all brief citations from his collection of columns, *The Truman Era*, which Pells uses only to flesh out descriptions of the "feel" of the times. (For other omissions from Pells's book, see David M. Oshinsky, "Before the Left Was New," New York *Times Book Review*, February 10, 1985. Oshinsky's review is also illuminating in that it shows how Pells's position on the inspiration of McCarthyism [which Oshinsky calls "poorly documented and probably untrue"] might have benefited from citations to Stone's work.) Even more mystifying is Stone's near-invisibility in a book that, by its authors' own admission, takes its title from Stone. Except for some recycled material on the founding of Students for a Democratic Society (SDS) and two minor references in *Who Spoke Up? American Protest Against the War in Vietnam, 1963–1975*, Nancy Zaroulis and Gerald Sullivan apparently do not consider Stone's one of the more important voices in this period.

I asked Stephen E. Ambrose, now Alumni Professor of History at the University of New Orleans and the distinguished biographer of Eisenhower and Nixon, if he could shed any light on Stone's absence from the literature of the Cold War revisionists. Ambrose stands out from the group that includes Gar Alperovitz, Walter LaFeber, Gabriel and Joyce Kolko, and William Appelman Williams in his acknowledgment of Stone's importance in his book *Rise to Globalism: American Foreign Policy Since 1938*. Was it that Stone had gone too far in his *Hidden History*, as has been suggested to me by Stanley Kutler of the University of Wisconsin, among others; or was it a vestige of some kind of McCarthyism, even among its opponents; or Stone's lack of academic credentials . . . "The latter," Ambrose interjected before I could offer any other possibilities. "Academic snobbery. No more or less than that." I mentioned my frustration in looking through book after book and article after article that had "arrived" at the same conclusions that Stone had come to many years earlier. "Sure," Ambrose said, "there are people who have made their reputations on observations that Stone had come out with years before who would never dream of citing Stone, simply because he's a journalist. Don't ever underestimate academic jealousy and you'll never go wrong."

Professor Ambrose himself may have provided an unfortunately apt epitaph for the *Hidden History* in his review of the 1969 reissue of Stone's Korean study, which ran in the Baltimore *Sun* (September 19, 1969) under the heading, "Destined to Be Ignored." Ambrose commented then, seventeen years after the book's initial publication, that Stone's "insights are valid, yet they have been ignored. What he first pointed out has since been routinely accepted by historians, but it has not reached the State Department [apropos of Vietnam], much less a wider public." Ambrose cited Stone's theses on the lack of Russian or Chinese involvement in the initial invasion; on MacArthur's "major, almost sole" role in continuing the war in 1950; and on the complicity between the Pentagon, MacArthur, and the South Koreans in allowing the initial North Korean attack. "Mr. Stone's only sin, however," Ambrose concluded, "was in being too honest too soon. . . . It took guts to publish this book in the McCarthy era. Today, millions are jumping on the bandwagon of damning our Asian policy—even President Nixon is climbing aboard. In 1952, Mr. Stone was a one-man band. It is a pity that more Americans did not read and think about *Hidden History* at that time." Nevertheless, eighteen years after that review, Stone's book remains ignored, or misrepresented.

Ambrose's assessment of *Hidden History* was not uncritical, however. He expressed reservations about Stone's suggestion that the South might have provoked the war in the first place, although he acknowledges that Stone's "circumstantial evidence is good" and that all of those who Stone said stood to benefit from the conflict—Rhee, Chiang, and Truman— "got what they wanted from the Korean War." Stone's work on Korea was also acknowledged by D. F. Fleming in *The Cold War and Its Origins* (1961), a book that has also been met with silence by later historians, again with the notable exception of Ambrose. Fleming called the *Hidden History* "an intriguing book written by an able, experienced newspaperman. It is based . . . entirely upon an analysis of published accounts and is a keen examination and collation of them. While many readers would not accept some of Stone's deductions, others cannot be ignored. The volume contains much food for thought."

Townsend Hoopes is one of the few who differ with Stone's

suggestions who at least acknowledges him in print. In *The Devil and John Foster Dulles* (1973), Hoopes also calls many of the points Stone raises "circumstantial." But his two chief arguments against Stone are themselves not very secure. Hoopes holds that the Russians were indeed involved in the planning of the North Korean attack on the South and that Stalin (and Mao) "blessed" Kim Il Sung's war plan. The only support he offers for his theory is a passage from Khrushchev's memoirs, and even Hoopes questions the reliability of this source: "But Khrushchev, if his account can be accepted, has demolished the vital point" of Stone's argument. Moreover, Hoopes believes that Dulles would never have cooperated in any of Syngman Rhee's machinations on the grounds that Dulles was a dove! Hoopes writes that, while Dulles "was no pacifist, most of his thinking and writing since Versailles had concentrated steadfastedly on the problem of how to prevent war." As Stone has demonstrated on numerous occasions from Dulles's own writings, his interest was in how to prevent war with Nazi Germany for most of this period. Hoopes is similarly naïve when he credits statements by Dulles appearing in the *Presbyterian Tribune* of October 1947, that "war is intolerable" and that "Christians must reject [it]."

Abroad, however, foreign critics have recently begun to acknowledge the importance of Stone's writings on the Korean War. Gavan McCormack in *Cold War, Hot War: An Australian Perspective on the Korean War* (Sydney, 1983) reminds us that Stone's book raised "questions which hardly anyone else was prepared to utter in 1952, or later." Kajimura Hideki likewise salutes its value as an "indispensible reference" thirty years on in *Chōsen gendaishi no tebiki* (Guide to Contemporary Korean History; Tokyo, 1981).

It is worthwhile to note that in the Malcolm Pittman Sharp Collection of the University of Chicago Law Library, the only two volumes selected by Sharp for the Cold War period are Stone's and Fleming's. Sharp, for many years professor of law at the University of Chicago, shared many of Stone's concerns, but perhaps because of background and upbringing, he was less hesitant to describe many of his cultural and political biases as conservative. The phrase he used on several occasions with me was that of Henry Adams: "a conservative Christian anarchist." Sharp also published an important book with Monthly Review Press, *Was Justice Done? The Rosenberg-Sobell Case* (1956), and had himself assisted the Rosenbergs' defense in the final appeals. Though Sharp's book met with a silence similar to that which greeted Stone's (due, in part, one suspects, to attitudes about its publisher), it is interesting to note that Ronald Radosh and Joyce Milton, in a bibliographic essay in their book *The Rosenberg File: A Search for Truth* (1984), find Sharp's the only contemporary account of the case that still stands as "honest and serious . . . calm, judicious, and carefully constructed."

Radosh and Milton are the only historians of *that* thorny controversy who are unafraid to discuss Stone's suggestions. They, too, open their book with a citation from the *Weekly*, and cite his reporting in the *Compass* and the *Weekly* as having been among those sources "most helpful" in their exhaustive review of the Rosenberg case.

Stone is also missing from most general histories of the nation's press, even those that chronicle the press in opposition. Edward R. Bayley's *Joe McCarthy and the Press* (1981) and Kathleen J. Turner's *Lyndon Johnson's Dual War: Vietnam and the Press* (1985), with its considerable bibliography, are but two of the more recent examples of this blindness. Stone is missing as well from many major accounts of the 1960s. Allen J. Matusow's *The Unraveling of America: A History of Liberalism in the 1960s* (1984) contains a single, almost gratuitous, reference to *I. F. Stone's Weekly* as the source for his characterization of Barry Goldwater's base of support in 1964.

This "chill" of Stone is especially bizarre in works on the sixties. During the Vietnam War, Stone's circulation was to rise from 20,000 in 1963 to 70,000 in 1971. His August 24, 1964 issue had taken on the Tonkin Gulf Resolution. His March 8, 1965, issue was given over to his influential piece, "A Reply to the White Paper," the first serious effort to refute the documentation of the State Department on the nature of the Southeast Asian conflict. And Stone played a key role in steering the newly formed SDS to a position of active opposition to the war, as well as securing SDS legitimacy among older, more established left-wing organizations. "By this time," Paul Booth recently told James Miller, "we . . . depended on him to interpret all the events of the world for us. The moment his *Weekly* arrived, we devoured it." (See *Democracy Is in the Streets: From Port Huron to the Siege of Chicago*, 1987.) His speech to the SDS National Council on December 29, 1964, was directly responsible for SDS's organization of the first major antiwar march on Washington, on April 17, 1965, according to Tom Hayden and other participants (see, for example, Irwin Unger, *The Movement*, 1974), and Stone was one of the chief speakers at the rally of 20,000 along with Alaska senator Ernest Gruening, his former editor at the New York *Post*.

There are usually exceptions that prove life's rules. As I was sitting one day staring at a stack of books that I was

scouring for mention of Stone or the *Weekly*, the spine of
Ronald Steel's *Walter Lippmann and the American Century* caught
my eye. Though I remembered having been quite impressed
with the book when I first read it, and though I was fully
aware of its reputation for exhaustive documentation, I also
knew that Steel had neglected Stone in his *Pax Americana*, and
that, of course, Lippmann was practically antipodal to Stone,
as much in his political philosophy as in his concern with status and "respectability." A quick glance at the index told me,
however, that I had found just what I was looking for even
before I actually looked up the citation. The book has 599 pages
of text and the Stone reference led me to page 576:

> As [Lippmann] grew more and more estranged from
> the [Johnson] administration, he began listening to
> some of the radical critics of the war. In the spring of
> 1966 he talked to leftist journalist Felix Greene, who
> had been to Hanoi, and at the home of Bernard Fall had
> dinner with radical newsman I. F. Stone, just returned
> from Saigon. Two weeks later, when the Lippmanns
> gave their annual mint julep party on the lawn, they in-
> vited "Izzy" and Esther Stone—a small gesture, but one
> that was noticed in the tight little Washington social
> world, where each guest list carried a political meaning.
> Even more noticeable than the presence of the Stones
> was the absence from the party of any important
> administration official. Lippmann, so long an insider,
> was now among the outsiders.

It was as if Walter Lippmann and I. F. Stone met at the
intersection of two arcs, one declining and one ascending.
Stone's position on the war had not changed, of course,

but Lippmann's perception that "acceptable" was not a legitimate qualifier for truth had. Stone's complaint against "respectability" is a frequent one, but Lippmann's shift on Vietnam and the subsequent decline of his social fortunes (and, might one add, his personal happiness?) would seem to give weight to Stone's concern.

It should also be noted that Lippmann's social "suffering" did not continue for long. Steel relates how Lippmann was courted by Bobby Kennedy and how, after RFK's assassination, he backed Nixon over Humphrey. Nixon subsequently wined and dined Lippmann, as did Kissinger, seeking advice and legitimacy. Though there is no denying a change in Lippmann as a result of Vietnam, it was no sea change. He was an old man, setting out on retirement. But the contrasts with Stone are still instructive: German Jew, Russian Jew; rich man, poor man; college man, dropout. As a boy, Stone may have read John Reed with delight; Lippmann had known him at Harvard. But it is hardly stretching things to look at the issue of self-creation here. Lippmann was a precocious young man, but he did a great deal with what he was given by family background as well. And his development really ceased in middle age. Retirement for him was travel and parties. The writing, and perhaps the thinking, ceased.

Woody Allen's 1983 film *Zelig* told the story of a man who had no characteristics of his own but had the ability to take on the personality—and even the physical appearance—of anybody he met. The film is in the style of a documentary and takes as its starting point the mysterious ubiquity in so many of the historical photographs and documents of the twenties of a now-forgotten figure. With I. F. Stone the situation is just the opposite: he is a kind of Zelig in reverse, notable for his *absence* from scenes where one would expect to find him. Perhaps the publication some day of a comprehensive biography will put him in a position of prominence, and assure that he will be given weight in future historical works. But something more will be needed to restore him to his rightful place as an observer, commentator, and participant in his times.

26

POEMS

And a second memory stands out: my father,
giving me, when I was ten, some Robinson Jeffers
to read, saying, "To be a great poet is the greatest
thing in the world."

> Celia Gilbert (I. F. Stone's daughter)
> "The Sacred Fire"
> in *Working It Out*, 1978
> (ed., Ruddick and Daniels)

ONE DAY, our lunch ended, we stepped out onto Nebraska
Avenue. Stone seemed uncomfortable about continuing our
discussions of "contemporary" politics, as he often did during my time with him. He wanted to get back to the Greeks.
He also wanted to get some groceries to take home to his
wife for dinner. Certain things seem to come to Stone as
naturally as breathing—the memorization and recollection of
poetry in a variety of languages, for example. And other
things that often confound the rest of us, such as shopping
for groceries or keeping our train of thought while crossing
a busy four-lane street—appear to him as minor nuisances
best ignored and at worst tolerated. No sooner had we hit
the pavement in search of salmon steaks than he was off on
the subject of Greek poetry.

"In my first Plato lecture I read a lot of Greek poetry and
translated it. Well received. Would you like an illustration

of the quality of Greek verse? This is one of them I use—by the way, I was looking up a favorite quatrain of mine by Blake. Do you like Blake? Do you know the one about—

> To see a World in a Grain of Sand
> And a Heaven in a Wild Flower,
> Hold Infinity in the palm of your hand
> And Eternity in an hour.

Isn't that wonderful? But I came across one I didn't remember, called 'The Fly.' Do you know that one?

> Little fly,
> Thy summer's play
> My thoughtless hand
> Has brush'd away.

> Am not I
> A fly like thee?
> Or art not thou
> A man like me?

> For I dance,
> And drink, and sing,
> Till some blind hand
> Shall brush my wing.

> If thought is life
> And strength and breath,
> And the want
> Of thought is death;

> Then am I
> A happy fly,

If I live
Or if I die.

Isn't that marvelous? I'll give you a sample of Greek poetry.
There's a Greek poem by Callimachus. He was a third
century [B.C.] Alexandrian poet and the translation of his
poem to another poet, his friend Heraclitus—not the philosopher—is one of the most famous translations of Greek
verse into English, done by a man named Cory. And maybe
you've heard it. The translation is this:

They told me, Heraclitus, they told me you were dead,
They brought me bitter news to hear and bitter tears to shed.
I wept as I remembered how often you and I
Had tired the sun with talking and sent him down the sky.

And now that thou art lying, my dear old Carian guest,
A handful of grey ashes, long, long ago at rest,
Still are thy pleasant voices, thy nightingales, awake;
For Death, he taketh all away, but them he cannot take.''

Bear in mind that we have just crossed the street and are
headed for the Giant supermarket. It has amazed me while
transcribing and editing my conversations with Stone that
they read like interviews conducted in some professor's
study, or perhaps in the private office of a retired executive,
or like the transcripts of a prepared lecture. That Stone
speaks in paragraphs and chapters is remarkable in itself.
That he does so while walking, eating, or running errands
is another thing entirely. Of course his obliviousness to
the external world is not without its occasional comic side.
I wonder what the other shoppers in the Giant that day

thought of the sight of an elderly man running up and down the aisles reciting Greek poetry while a young man with a tape recorder and a note pad ran at his heels trying to capture the man's speech over the din of Muzak, chatter, and the check-out line.

"That is a pretty good translation. But the original far surpasses it. First of all, the translation is a jingle. And there are a lot of lines that are artificial—to keep the meter, to keep the rhyme."

The Muzak is swelling now. I'm thinking that any "jingle" of this guy Cory "far surpasses" the jingle I hear in the frozen food section.

"Now the Greek original is a four-line elegiac hexameter. It's a quatrain of four lines—I don't think we need a shopping cart—the Homeric line, the hexameter. It has six feet. The elegiac hexameter is a favorite form of the Greeks. The odd-numbered lines, the first and the third, are a plain elegiac Homeric dactylic hexameter. But the even-numbered lines are made up of the halves of a dactylic hexameter repeated, but with the last part of the syllable knocked off. So you have the two halves put together into what's called a *pent*ameter. But it's not *really* a pentameter. So it gives a little bump at the middle."

The Muzak swells, as if on a perverse cue. "I'll tell you what the original says. The original is far superior to the translation. I'll give you the Greek so you can hear the Greek a little bit. It says *Eipe tis*, ["Shoppers, please note: the aisle scales are provided for your use, but they do not always give exact weights."] 'Someone told me' ["That's right, this scale is only for estimates."] *Hēracleite*, 'Heraclitus,' *teon moron*, 'of your fate, of what happened to you.'

Es de me dakry ēgagen, 'it drew a tear from me.' [The Muzak is really rising now.] That's the first line. ["Register number six will now open."] Looking for some small apples. Let's go back here . . . *Emnēsthēn d' hossakis amphoteroi,* 'I remembered how often you and I, *hēlion en leschē,* 'the sun in his bed,' *katedysamen*—'how often we had put the sun to sleep in his bed.' *Alla sy men pou,* 'but now somewhere,' *xein Halikarnēseu*—that means 'my guest-friend from Halicarnassus.' In that translation that's called 'Carian' because the city of Halicarnassus was in the province of Caria in Asia Minor. *Tetrapalai spodiē,* 'long, long ago—a handful of dust,' *ai de teai zōousin aēdones,* 'thy nightingales still live.' *Ēisin ho pantōn harpaktēs Haidēs,* 'but Hades, the robber god'—I'm extending a little—'the robber god of the underworld who snatches away all things' ["Let's watch out for those carts there. "], *ouk epi cheira balei,* 'will never lay his hands upon them.'

"You can see the delicacy of the Greek, compared to that jingle. I spoiled the rhythm a little bit by breaking up the words. Otherwise, you'd be hearing gibberish without any explanation. And I want to use that method to transmit the quality of the content.

"There's a poem of Sappho's about a rival whom she consigns to hell. And there are two translations of it that are well known. One by Thomas Hardy, who was quite a good poet as you know, and another by Swinburne; the Swinburne translation is very lush and the Hardy is very austere. And they're both very good poems. How much is that? ["$9.77."] But the original has a splendid directness and an immediacy that the translations don't have at all. Thank you. Norwegian salmon, it's very good.

[Beeeeeeeep!] Tell you one more elegiac hexameter if you'd like to hear one. There's a four-line elegiac hexameter—are these doors automatic?—which appears in the *Oxford Book of Greek Verse* as "On a Tombstone in Tarm." And it's in the *Penguin Book of Greek Verse*, edited by Professor Trypanis, a marvelous book. It goes from Homer to Elytis—straight through the Byzantine period. And like the other Penguin books of foreign verse, it has the best thing of all, a simple, plain, prose translation at the bottom of the page. It helps you understand the Greek and it doesn't deform it by squeezing it into the meters of another language. So this poem—Trypanis calls it "On Sabinis"—it took me quite a while to work it out. But when I got it, it's just beautiful. I'll try to transmit it to you. I'll give you the first two lines, 'cause they go together:

> *Touto toi hēmeterēs mnēmēion, esthle Sabine,*
> *hē lithos hē mikrē, tēs megalēs philiēs*

'This memorial, noble Sabinus, is only a stone,' *hē lithos hē mikrē,* 'and a little one at that'—you know, a small one. The Greek is so concise you have to add a few words to make it understandable—'to communicate so great a friendship as ours.' *Aiei zētēsō se*—oh, to understand the last line, you gotta understand that when the dead came to Hades and crossed the River Styx, they came to the fountain of Lethe. *Lēthēs* means forgetfulness, and they drank of the fountain and forgot their past life. So the last two lines say, 'I shall always search for you.' That's the literal meaning. Not 'long,' or 'long for.' As usual, in translating Greek the literal meaning is the best. 'I shall always search for you.' It doesn't make sense if you make it 'long for.' *Sy d', ei themis*, 'and of you'—*themis* is the main word in Homer for 'lawful' or 'proper'—'and if it be proper or lawful of you,' *en phthimenoisi*, 'down there among the departed' . . . And the last line's like a pearl necklace, it's exquisite. It has a genitive at the beginning, a genitive article. And in between are two qualifying phrases deftly woven in to fit the meter. And it goes *Tou Lēthēs ep' emoi mē ti pieis ydatos*. He says, 'If it be proper, please, for my sake, do not drink—even a drop—of the waters of forgetfulness.' Isn't that beautiful? Isn't that beautiful? The Greek poets are just marvelous.

"And, you know, Homer—Homer in translation is just a big mishmash of war and mythology. But in the original—what an artist! What artistry, what magic! What magic! What magic! No translation really can transmit it. You look at it and you think how did he *do* it? What's the magic? How did he say so much? He's like Gide or Picasso, doing a lot with a single stroke, with a word. It's the fruit not of a barbarous, but of a very cultivated age. And it has a splendid directness. There's no cloying or pretty-pretty poetry. You know what I mean? And everything comes out of Homer: the tragic poets and the lyric poets and the oratory. It's all in Homer, all there in Homer. It's amazing. All of Greek literature really grows out of Homer.

"I don't read Modern Greek. I'm dying to be able to read the Modern Greek. I can recognize certain terms. For example, in the great Chorus on Man in Sophocles' *Antigone*, there you have the word *astynomos*, the law of the city in ancient times. And I'm delighted to find that in Modern Greek, *astinomos* means the town cop. 'The law,' as we say. *Asty* is town—not *polis*, a little bit broader than *polis*—and *nomos* is law or custom.

"I enjoy working with those Penguin books. I have the ones on Greek verse, Latin, Hebrew, French, Japanese, German. You see it's good to work on the short poems. I'll tell you why. Because it's not as complicated as when you tackle a long sentence, and you get the satisfaction— you work on a two-line couplet, but still it's not an endless task. You look up every word and you get it and you see the translation and you get the rhythm.

> *Andra moi ennepe, Mousa, polytropon, hos mala polla*
> *planchthē, epei Troiēs hieron ptoliethron eperse:*
> *pollōn d' anthrōpōn iden astea kai noon egnō*

"All of Greek civilization is in those first three lines of the *Odyssey*. When he says 'Muse, sing me that man *polytropon*'—which can mean either much tossed about or it can mean a man of versatile character, a many-sided man— 'who suffered so much after he sacked the holy citadel of Troy, and he saw so many men and got to understand their minds.' *Noon* is the accusative singular of *noos*, mind, and *egnō* is from *gignōskō*, the verb 'to know.' Everything is very compact in Homer. You see, *tropos* can mean character and *poly* means many, many-character—it means you're many-sided, versatile. Or it can have to do with being tossed about.

"You see, in poetry, the form and the content are indissoluble, and something that is imperishably beautiful in one language can be quite banal and even pedestrian when it's translated literally into another language. Because you don't have the same music, the same reverberations of the words, the same connotations. I would love to be able to read the Chinese poets, for example. When I was a boy, I read all the translations that I could get my hands on. It must be very, very hard, Chinese."

OWEN LATTIMORE

"I was a good friend of Owen's. He had a kind of Chinese Studies institute, so he was able to operate in his chosen field [after his McCarthy-era troubles]. He's a great scholar of China and Mongolia. My first contact with him was during the Japanese attack on Manchuria; I was a young editorial writer on the Philadelphia *Record* and then the New York *Post*, and I read Lattimore's book *Manchuria: Cradle of Conflict*. It's a very good book, particularly in the psychology of the Chinese who made the jump of going beyond the Great Wall and overcoming the feeling of insecurity that it gave them and gaining psychic strength and feeling they had *done* it, they had gotten across the Great Wall. The difference between the psychology of the Manchurian Chinese and the rest of the country—an interesting insight. I always tried in my editorial work to do extra reading to get extra perspective."

27

BIOGRAPHY

IN ATTEMPTING a biography of Stone, a writer would encounter a peculiar obstacle, for Stone is a master autobiographer. In an introduction to a collection of his articles, as well as in an essay in the closing issue of the *Weekly*, and in a wonderful self-interview in the New York *Times Magazine* several years after his retirement, Stone has set down the essential facts of his life and the development of his philosophy in a form that is accurate, entertaining, and challenging to the reader. For the most part, efforts by the authors of two doctoral theses to supply new biographical information have merely filled in some of the chronological gaps. But I believe some additional insights into Stone's character are possible if one looks at his own *biographical* writings to see what they say about their author.

In particular, Stone's 1965 appreciation "The Pilgrimage of Malcolm X" is also an illuminating piece of autobiography. Only Stone would write an obituary analysis of Malcolm X using the insights of William James and Tertullian on the psychology of conversion or quoting from Xenophanes of Colophon on the anthropology of race and religion. And perhaps only Stone could get away with it. But the essay is fascinating for more than reasons of style or method.

Stone admires Malcolm because he, like Stone, is a self-made man, and by that I, of course, do not mean that he was some kind of financial success but that he had literally made himself through self-education, through reading, through action and experience, and through reflection. "He was a vicious prisoner," Stone wrote of Malcolm, "often in solitary. The other prisoners nicknamed him 'Satan.' But the prison had an unusually well-stocked library to which he was introduced by a fellow prisoner, an old-time burglar named Bimbi. Through him, Malcolm first encountered Thoreau. Prison became his university . . ."

The world, for Stone, seems divided into two kinds of people, or at least two kinds of people that draw his interest, the first for admiration, the second for sharp criticism: those who have seen in their lives the possibility of helping others and those who have turned their backs on their own development as socially conscious beings, and hence on their own human potential. In prison he "first encountered Thoreau," he writes of the young Malcolm Little. Stone is concerned with such encounters, and whether and how they shape people. In Stone's own case, they were frequent and lasting.

Stone sees an almost radical equality of opportunity in reading. His most dismissive comments are reserved for the bigoted and the small-minded, whom he sees as operating out of ignorance, and for the well-to-do and the powerful who have squandered their opportunities for self-development and service. His faith in the possibilities of individual growth seems unshakeable. "In the prison library Malcolm X was finding substantiation for the Black Muslim creed in *Paradise Lost* and Herodotus; this passionate curiosity and voracious reading were bound to make him outgrow Elijah [Muhammad]'s dream-book theology." But Stone does recognize the role of circumstance in his description of "the agony of this brilliant Negro's self-creation" as well.

Stone accepts Malcolm's diagnosis of the ills of Black America. But like a guide maneuvering his party through difficult terrain, Stone is mindful of the perils of the passage while he points out the beauty and importance of the sights. For example, while identifying the use of race hatred among the Black Muslims as a method for inculcating self-respect, he will accept no apology for racism: "There are passages in the *Autobiography of Malcolm X* in which Malcolm . . . sounds like a Southern white supremacist in reverse. . . . Black racism is still racism, with all its primitive irrationality and danger."

Stone attempts to place Malcolm and the Black Muslims in a context of world events and history. He draws attention to Malcolm's clever comparison in the *Autobiography* of the links between American Jews and World Jewry and the need and potential for links between Afro-Americans and "the world's Pan-Africanists." From Vittorio Lanternari's *The Religions of the Oppressed: A Study of Modern Messianic Cults*, Stone borrows the observation that the Black Muslims can be seen as a part of a worldwide phenomenon. "To see the Black Muslims and Malcolm's life in this perspective is to begin to understand the psychic havoc wrought around the world by white imperialism in the centuries since America was discovered and Afro-Asia opened up to white penetration. There are few places on earth where whites have not grown rich robbing the colored races. It was Malcolm's great contribution to help make us all aware of this."

But it was Malcolm's pilgrimage to Mecca that positioned him for what in Stone's eyes might have been his period of greatest influence. "New disillusions and a richer view of the human condition lay ahead for the man who could say, . . . 'Once they excluded the white man, they found they could get together.' " Malcolm was to see that "fratricide does not end with the eviction of the white devil." "It is tantalizing to speculate on what he might have become had he lived," Stone concludes.

Stone's appreciation of biography, and especially of intellectual biography, may seem to put him in an awkward position for an advocate of the socialist economic and political system. Stone is often aware of this apparent inconsistency. His frequent observations on "limits"—of action, of circumstances, even of analysis—are directed as much at himself as they are at others. Stone speaks frequently of a "fusion of Jefferson and Marx." But the examples of both his writing and his career would seem to put the importance of Jeffersonianism before that of Marxism. Certainly the occasions of his advocacy of increased Jeffersonianism in the Soviet bloc outnumber his suggestions of more Marxism in the United States. And while Stone endorses Malcolm X's description of the conditions of black Americans and his critique of the American power structure, does he not also accept implicitly the strengths that black Americans might find in Western ideas and ideals despite the years of "white imperialism"?

The men that Stone admires are independent thinkers, often anarchistic in their politics, but disciplined, and even sublime, in their thought. Those he most admires are what Emerson called "representative men," symbols or standards to be held up—Milton, Thoreau, Jefferson, Kropotkin. Then come the standard-bearers, those who take ideas and run with them. His obituary comments on two of these men, Henry Wallace and Alexander Meiklejohn, are instructive.

Stone was a supporter of Henry Wallace's 1948 presidential bid. But on the occasion of Wallace's death in 1965 he wrote, "Henry Wallace was an exasperating cross between a saint and a village innocent. He never gave to his work as a political leader or editor the kind of hard grappling with fact that he applied to his work as a corn breeder." This was not to renounce the ideals that Wallace stood for. Far from it; Stone still saw Wallace as a visionary from the perspective of twenty years after Wallace's candidacy. Food for Peace, full employment goals, peaceful coexistence with the Soviet Union, and Wallace's perception of a "century of the common man" were all testimony to Wallace's understanding of the difficulties that faced the United States in the prominence that it achieved after the Second World War. It was, rather, Wallace's failure to grasp either the sentiment of the country or the machinery of his own campaign that so exasperated Stone. Although Stone has always shown a preference for "ideal" candidates for the presidency, he has brought a degree of realism to left-of-center analysis, from his floating of the slogan "Back Ike for Peace" before the 1956 campaign, to his comments on British television in 1984 that Walter Mondale could not beat Reagan because, "Face it, you need *oomph* to be president."

In his assessment of the life of educator and civil libertarian Alexander Meiklejohn, Stone was chiefly concerned with what manner of man he was. "Few men have combined such deep convictions with such courtesy towards opposing points of view, such foreboding about man's fate with so sweet a serenity and so ever-fresh a joy." Stone salutes Meiklejohn's commitment to an absolute interpretation of the First Amendment and his combination of idealism with tolerance. Perhaps along the way Stone is also acknowledging the limits of politics and the conflicts between personal fulfillment and success in the political arena.

28

HOME

IN 1929 STONE MARRIED Esther Roisman. He had met her "on a borrowed dollar and a blind date." They have three children: Jeremy, a mathematician, is the director of the Federation of American Scientists and an expert on disarmament issues; Christopher is a professor of law at the University of Southern California; and Celia (Gilbert) is a published poet.

"Hi!"

"Esther, meet—"

"Yes, what a surprise!"

"Meet Andrew Patner."

"It's so nice to meet you."

"So, look, I got salmon, that nice Norwegian salmon, the same kind."

"Oh, Izzy, you're just an angel! What a good provider."

"And I got the apples. Any calls or anything?"

"Listen, somebody called and said you're in the Republican Party. Did you vote in the Republican Party?"

"Naaaw."

"They want you to help the Republicans."

"It's crazy. Last night I threw away a letter that began 'Fellow Republican.' "

"Yeah, well then somebody has you on the list as a Republican."

"Tell 'em I'm not."

"Well, I said you weren't. They said—you can't *imagine* how indignant the woman was. She says, 'I have him here! And I want him to vote for the chairman,' or something, and . . ."

"Well, tell them the last Republican I liked was Abraham Lincoln. Hey, I bought another bag of those small apples."

"Do you think they're good enough, Iz?"

"Yeah, absolutely."

29

TODAY

Stone is critical of today's emphasis on "professional" training for young journalists. He feels that journalism schools produce people "who know how to run a type-writer," but not how to research or think independently. He told me that he had talked to a young journalist who had never heard of Milton's *Areopagitica*. I suggested that he was lucky to have found one who had heard of Milton.

"They don't like to read," he said. "They don't even read the papers, that's the thing that gets me. I don't know where they get their ideas. It's awful. It's pathetic. It's the general decay of the educational system."

But Stone still admires the young people of another generation. "Oh, well, I *liked* the New Left crowd because they were—they didn't want everything neatly packaged for them. They were willing to face difficult problems, problems that were insoluble. Most problems are not soluble. You just learn to live with them. And they were quite unlike their parents and grandparents. They weren't looking for a simple ideology which would solve everything. Most of them weren't. They were willing to improvise and just do their thing. And I liked them for that. There were in the New Left, of course, vestiges of all the different splinter movements. You know, Progressive Labor came out of it. They're very Stalinist. But in general, the New Left movement was fresh and *re*freshing, I thought."

But wasn't much of this going against what Stone has said about the importance of history? Weren't the New Left activists advocates of an unrealistic discontinuity?

"Some of it. In the movie—in Jerry's movie—there's a place where I scold the kids for not learning more history."

I reminded Stone that in the movie, he told the young people that protest for its own sake was like a child banging its head on the floor when it's frustrated. "It may be therapeutic," he had suggested, "but is it politics?"

"Oh, did I say that? It's very good."

And hadn't many of the leaders of that generation—Jane Fonda, Jerry Rubin—and many of their followers as well, the yuppies and so forth, sold out in the end? Weren't there some tendencies in that direction?

"I don't know. I don't like to sit in judgment. They were a bunch of good kids. They were like a breath of fresh air. So some of them fell by the wayside. What the hell? You see, one point: these were the children of the affluent, revolting against affluence. Against the mindless affluence of their parents. Working like hell for nothing. For ulcers. For new cars every year. For worthless things. It was a revolt against middle-class affluence. *Mindless* affluence. I think of them as a wonderful generation."

30

PROGRESS

"HERE ARE THE REMAINS of my first paper."

"Oh, so this is the *Progress*, from when you were a boy."

"I have a few of these covered in plastic."

"So even in your first paper, in your very first paper, you have Sophocles!"

"Did I?" Stone chuckles. "I forgot that!" He chuckles again.

"Yes, it's something from *Antigone*: 'Nothing in use by man for power of ill can equal money.' "

"Oh! That's a real radical quote. I'll be darned! I'll be darned! So I was reading the Greek stuff *then*! In translation."

"So it's come full circle?"

"Yes, I guess it has.

"These are the last surviving copies, all the pages. I ran it with Gerhardt van Arckle, a friend of mine in high school. He later became general counsel to the National Labor Relations Board. He died just recently here in Washington. He was my oldest friend. He was quite friendly to me during the witch hunt, when he was 'respectable' and I was not. You can see it was a political paper."

I began to read from another page of Stone's childhood *Progress*.

" 'A Nut-E Poem by An Animus, Poetic License No. 1239':

When the whales of Wales wails,
Before the ship sails at sales of Sales,
They buy sails . . ."

"Who wrote that? I hope it wasn't me!"
"Look! You had advertising!"

INDEPENDENCE

"Independence is always important in any society to combat the establishment mind. I have more stuff in print than any journalist of my time. And really, I think this stuff has made a contribution to the literature of American journalism. And I don't think many people have written that well. These big establishment figures—not that I'm against them, but I think my stuff is going to last longer than they can."

31

RETIREMENT

When he retired as a political columnist nine years ago, [Alsop] devoted himself to art history and published a scholarly work called *The Rare Art Traditions: A History of Art Collecting and Its Linked Phenomena.* . . . Now he has begun compiling materials for his memoirs. . . .

In the Vietnam War, Alsop was a hawk and he still thinks of it as a war "we could have won and should have won" if President Lyndon B. Johnson had made strong patriotic appeals instead of trying "to make a war without the *New York Times* noticing."

Despite his assertions that he is passé, Alsop is still among the annointed at the intimate dinners that are the hallmarks of the city's social and power games. "Your place at the table changes rather," he said, focusing for a moment on Washington's social anthropology, "and that's as it should be. It's much harder to make new friends. You can't just call and say, 'I'm Joe Alsop. I live on N Street. Would you like to come and have a drink.' "

"It's been my observation that you go on living like a young man until suddenly you're an old man," he said. "It's a bore. There's absolutely nothing to recommend old age. It's a great deal

easier if you have a pleasant house and a good
cook, which is no doubt the result of unfairness
and inequality. But so be it. As long as it lasts
. . ." Then with a laugh, he lights another cigarette and says: "You never like what you are not
used to when you're old."

William E. Farrell
"Chatting with Acerbic Joseph Alsop"
International Herald-Tribune
October 30, 1984

"THIS IS MY GREEK and Latin library. This is a very good
edition of Aristotle's *Nicomachean Ethics*, because it has a glos-
sary for non-Greek readers explaining the key conceptual
terms. This is a lexicon of Platonic terms, it's in French. This
is indispensable for the *Republic*, a commentary on the mono-
logues; supplementary essays too. Now, this edition of the
Republic, by Allan Bloom—I don't agree with the interpretation at all, but what's useful about it is the exegesis he gives
of the philosophical terms. That's very useful. There are all
the works of my hero Grote. That's his three volumes on
Plato, his posthumous *Aristotle*, his *History of Greece* in twelve
volumes. Here are a lot of basic commentaries. This one is
very hard to get. I got it for $1.25. I said, 'You got any
Greek stuff?' He said, 'I got a whole box full of it upstairs.'
This is a very famous Oxford scholar who died young. He
would have had a great career. It has a very useful appendix
on the idioms of Plato, a very useful essay on the *daimonion*
and Socrates. Very useful. When you're working alone, without a teacher, you need a lot of commentaries.

"This is *very* good. In fact, I think it's the best translation of the *Apology* because . . . English and French make Plato sound a little more direct than he really is. I don't mean to say he's cumbersome, he's not. But German captures the subtle nuances and patterns. Here's the greatest commentary on the *Timaeus*, by Thomas Taylor, the English neo-Platonist. This is the Bohn Plato. This is the first edition of Jowett, and the third edition with a lot of supplementary materials. This is my complete Philo and here's a complete Loeb Library Plato. This is an almost complete Aristotle. I'm only missing two volumes for a complete set. This is a wonderful commentary by Newman on the *Politics*. This is Jowett's *Politics*. It's not especially wonderful, but it has a marvelous analytical index. I bought it for the index. People don't make good indexes any more. An analytical index is a big help, especially in such a rich work as the *Politics*, a real labyrinth. This book here has a wonderful Greek index and an English index. This is my great prize. [He brings down a heavy old volume.] This is the first printing of the first translation ever made of Plato—by Marsilio Ficino, the great Florentine mystic. I found it in a bookstore here in Washington fifteen years ago. It's not in good condition, but it's all there, all of Plato. Let's see, what year is this?"

And it is here that the observer is drawn back to physical reality. For one can walk with Stone for hours, listen to him talk, or read his works, all the time forgetting that he is nearly blind. He has always suffered from weak vision, and now, in recent years, he has a cataract in one eye and a detached retina in the other. He lifts the book to his "good eye" and pulls it back and forth slowly across his face, often making out sentences one word at a time—and words, one letter at a time. But his vision has never been an excuse to read or work less, nor is he open to much sympathy on his condition.

"It's 1546, at Basle," I read.

"Marsilio also translated Plotinus," Stone continues. "This is my New Testament lexicon. This is my Septuagint, very useful. This is the most famous commentary on the *Agamemnon*. This is all of Plutarch. All the *Moralia* and all the *Lives*. Some of the commentaries. Marvelous. And here's a lot of Aristotle. This is Eduard Zeller's *History of Greek Philosophy*. I don't have a complete set, but the remaining ones I have xeroxed. This is Guthrie, who is rather commonplace.

"Now, I've collected an awful lot of schoolbook editions of plays, because working alone you need a lot of help when you do the plays. There's a real treasure, in bad condition, but this is the old Bohn library. A literal translation of all the Greek plays—Aristophanes, Sophocles, Euripides, and Aeschylus. Here's the Oxford classical text of all the playwrights. And here's a lot of Latin stuff. This is the most wonderful translation of Plotinus—done by an Irish newspaperman who gave up his work and devoted his whole life to it. When I was a boy at school, the first of the nine *Enneads* had just appeared separately and I read it without the Greek with great enthusiasm. It was beautiful. This is the Guillaume Budé three volumes of Plotinus. And this is the new Loeb edition of Plotinus. They've brought out three more volumes. I've got a lot of Cicero. I've got all of Pliny, quite a few of the historians. I have some works on science.

"Here's a lot more Greek stuff. This is my Homeric. This is the complete Guillaume Budé, beautiful typography. This is the three different commentaries, two on the *Iliad* and one on the *Odyssey*. Professor Stanford's edition. Wonderful edition. I met him on a tour of the Greek Islands once. This is Gilbert Murray's history of the Greek epic. Here's all of Aristophanes. And here's a nice rarity: this is an edition by a famous nineteenth-century scholar of the scholia. They're the notes on the margins of the ancient manuscripts, glosses that help you understand. Now, the *Clouds*, which is important for Socrates—I have about four different commentaries, including this by K. J. Dover. Here is my Thucydides library. I've got a complete set of the great Gomme's commentary. This is Hobbes's Thucydides. This is Jowett's Thucydides and commentary. This is the Modern Library's Thucydides, and these are other Thucydides. This is some of North's Plutarch, the one Shakespeare used. This is a work by Parrington. He was an independent left-liberal scholar, self-taught, at Liverpool. He's fallen out of favor in this age. Here are works by Finley, Adkins.

"This is all classical scholarship. This is the *Pauly-Wissowa*, the *Kleine Pauly*, in five volumes. The most voluminous encyclopedia of classical learning is the German *Pauly-Wissowa*. It's about twenty-five volumes, done by a whole army of scholars, and this is the little one, in five volumes. It's easier to read because they can't have such long sentences. This is a history of classical scholarship. Here's Professor Constantine Trypanis's enormous book on Greek verse, from Homer to Seferis. Here are a lot of the plays, and here's a complete *Greek Anthology*. Symonds's *Greek Poets*. Complete Pindar in French and English. Complete Hesiod. The *Greek Anthology*, complete in different versions. Here's Trypanis's Penguin book. I've worn mine out, there's so many things in there I've worked on. See, there's the Sappho poem. There's the *Oxford Book of Greek Verse*. *The Oxford Book of Latin*

Verse. This is a wonderful commentary on the *De rerum natura* of Lucretius by the great American poet William Ellery Leonard, who taught at Wisconsin. This is very interesting, Diels's *Fragments of the Pre-Socratics*. It's the original fascicle of Heraclitus. I bought this as a boy when my favorite Greek teacher died. The date is 1927, the year I quit college. I bought his Liddell and Scott too. I have a number of collections of pre-Socratics. This is one of the best. It gives you the complete Greek text and the expositions. A lot of miscellaneous treasures there.

"The thing is, I've got a well-stocked library here. I can check out references, cross references, right away instead of going downtown to the library.

"This is my Marxist and Russian stuff—oh, this is a memoir, never translated. I thought I'd get it translated. In English it would be *The Story of a Frustrated Peace*—it's by Jean Sainteny, published in France in 1953. He was in DeGaulle's cabinet later. He negotiated with Ho Chi Minh to stay in the French Union after the war. It tells the story of how the French broke the pact. I really read that thoroughly. All of Marx's *Capital*. Here's Rosa Luxemburg, Trotsky, Bukharin, Alexander Herzen's memoirs, complete. This is my Chinese stuff. Here are the remains of my seventeenth-century studies. Clarendon's *History of the Rebellion*. I still try to enrich my knowledge in that period. There's a *U.S. Code and Constitution Annotated*. And there's a big fat volume of Madison's *Notes* and all the other notes on the Constitutional Conventions. That's Crosskey's *Politics and the Constitution*. Quite a man.

"These are all quite rare classical works that exist only in libraries today. I check them out of the Library of Congress and xerox them. This is one on the trial of Socrates. French.

"That's a reading machine. The guy who did the movie about me, Jerry Bruck, bought it for me. It's really for—I'm not quite blind enough yet to use it, but it's nice to have. See that? It zooms in . . . to look at one letter! You can just have one letter on the whole screen! This is the unabridged Liddell and Scott. Here's the fourteenth edition of the *Encyclopaedia Britannica*. It's better than the new ones. Here are the two great Jefferson biographies of the nineteenth century. This is Campbell's little-known work on the pilgrim fathers in Holland, England, and America. There are the anti-Federalists. There's a lot of my Jewish stuff. Gershom Scholem—I've got all of his stuff. And there's a wonderful book on the Christian Hasidim. I've been looking for a good Jewish book on the New Testament. There's my *Facts on File*, which I have all the way back to the beginning. It's quite good. It was very helpful. That's my Bible collection. This is a complete Soncino Bible. Here's a *chumash* in a beautiful edition with Hebrew and English and commentary. And this is a Zohar. And this is Rashi's *chumash*. It has the Hebrew and it has the Targum in the Aramaic of Onkelos. This is Harry Austryn Wolfson. The great Wolfson. I once spent an afternoon with him in the Widener Library. Philo. Philo's a wonderful writer. But you know, the rabbis frown on the Hebrew philosophers. Philo was on the border. Maimonides had his books burned. Spinoza was kicked out of the synagogue. This is all of Bertrand Russell. I was invited to contribute to a *Festschrift* for him. And I collected all of his books to get ready. The assignment scared me. The book, *Philosopher of the Century*, was hardly circulated in this country. He was wonderful. His *History of Western Philosophy* is a potboiler, but it's wonderful. I later did a study of the relationship between mathematics and mysticism from Pythagoras to Russell. Up there is Henry C. Lea's history of the Spanish Inquisition and his history of the medieval inquisition. Works on witchcraft. He was a great American scholar. This is my old Loesser Bible, from my *bar mitzvah*. These are bound volumes of the *New York Review*. All scholars sneer at this—the Durant series—but they're quite wrong. It's awfully good. Worth having. I know a little bit about the Greek stuff, and it's very good. But he's a radical and a Jew and a progressive. And they're just jealous of anybody . . .

"Here's my medieval stuff. All of St. Augustine. The church fathers, Jewish stuff. This is some of my philosophy. This is my Graetz *History of the Jews*, from my *bar mitzvah*. Here's another book from my boyhood. I had six years of Latin. This is all the Latin poets with French translation. I got this as a boy. I was a philosophy major, you see. Here's one of the first books I ever bought. I paid two dollars as a boy for this, Milman's edition of Gibbon. I love Gibbon. This is the complete works of Dionysius the Areopagite. And here it is in French. A very important figure for medieval studies.

"It's so much fun to be learning, to have the leisure to learn and study. Every night I look things up, cross references, encyclopedias. Here, these are my note cards for my lectures. Take a look at them and you'll get some sense of how it's organized. ["Socrates," "Plato: Non-rational side," "Conscience," "Lecture One: Virtue and Knowledge: Nature of Knowledge and Virtue," "Socrates as a pro-Spartan," "Nature of human society," "Contempt for affairs of the city," "Withdrawal from politics," "Socrates as snob."]

"You see, I break them down into analytical subpoints. I have a file for each lecture and then a pack of cards for each point and I review them before each talk. But when I give the talk, I never look at them. I review them thoroughly before, but I don't use anything at the lectern because I don't really see well enough. I have to stick it up my nose. And anyway, I have much more than I need. It's very good to face an audience. You get to the point faster. And I remember. I've been over the stuff now five times and it melds in your mind. It coalesces.

"Now I haven't *read* all of these books, but I'm familiar with them. I know how to use them, you know what I mean, the way a lawyer uses books. You don't memorize all the codes, you know where to look.

"Here are Paul Shorey's summaries of the dialogues. And Taylor's. This is Taylor's *Republic*, a marvelous work of scholarship. He's a Christian Platonist, a bit of an anti-Semite, and a terrible reactionary, but a wonderful scholar. And here's Josephus, Demosthenes. Jowett's *Life and Letters*. Here's a great Scandinavian scholar, Frisch. This is a Homeric reader . . . So I *really* have a well-stocked library. I can do an awful lot of research right here. In the evening, right out of bed. Here is all of Herodotus, including commentaries. Herodotus is *beautiful* in Greek; he's mellifluous. This is all of Polybius, who's very, very interesting. There's interesting work in there on the federal systems in Greece. You know the founding fathers were influenced by Polybius. In the *Federalist* there are references to Polybius. This is a wonderful analytical dictionary of Homer—every usage, it's just marvelous. If you start Greek, you must get yourself one. Homer's not hard. You'd be surprised. When I started out, it took me a whole evening in bed to do [laughs] a line and a half! And then, before the year was over, I was doing eighty lines a night. That's when I switched to Aeschylus. I read the *Prometheus*.

"I have so much pleasure! I spend an evening doing Greek or studying, and I just get out of bed feeling rejuvenated. Just rejuvenated! The Greek poets are just so wonderful. Oh, I'll tell you what plays I've done. I did the *Prometheus Bound* of Aeschylus, then I did the *Hecuba* of Euripides. Then I did *Oedipus Rex*, then I did the *Oresteia*, then I did the *Persians* of Aeschylus. Did the *Philoctetes* of Sophocles—a wonderful play. How good comes out of evil, evil out of good. I did the *Birds* of Aristophanes, and I'm halfway through the *Clouds*. You want to see a beautiful piece of early English printing? This is Xenophon's *Memorabilia of Socrates*. Greek text. It's a *cursive* Greek text and a Latin translation. What's the date?"

"Seventeen forty-one."

"Yeah. Isn't that a beautiful edition? Let's go back to your interview. So tell me, how much do you need?"

POSTLUDE

In the *Weekly* dated August 8, 1955, Stone published a "Note to the Rest of the Universe":

"Within two years you may see a flaming ball rocket up from the earth's surface and swing into position in an orbit around it. Do not regard the spectacle with complacency. These satellites will grow larger and more numerous; men will go up with them. Voyages to the moon will follow. After that the distant realm of planet and star will lie open to Man.

"Beware in time. This is a breed which has changed little in thousands of years. The cave dweller who wielded a stone club and the man who will soon wield an interstellar missile are terribly alike. Earth's creatures feed upon each other, but this is the only one that kills on a large scale, for pleasure, adventure and even—so perverse is the species—for supposed reasons of morality.

"Should you start a secret mission of inquiry, you will find that the sacred books on which the young of the various tribes have been brought up for thousands of years glorify bloodshed. Whether one looks in Homer, or the Sagas, or the Bible, or the Koran, the hero is a warrior. Someone is always killing someone else for what is called the greater glory of God.

"This is not a creature to be trusted with the free run of the universe. At the moment the human race seems to be temporarily sobered by the possession of weapons which could destroy all life on earth except perhaps the mosses and the fungi. The currently rival tribes, the Russians and the Americas, fear the other may use the new device against them. They may soon be transferring to outer space the hates that in every generation have brought suffering to the earth. It might be wise to stop them now, on the very threshold of the open and as yet unpolluted skies."

ABOUT THE AUTHOR

Andrew Patner, a staff reporter for *The Wall Street Journal*, graduated from the Chicago public schools, was editor-in-chief of the *Chicago Maroon* at the College of the University of Chicago, received a B.A. in history from the University of Wisconsin, and went on to attend the University of Chicago Law School. A former editor of *Chicago* magazine, he won the Peter Lisagor Award in 1983 for his coverage of race and politics in that city. He has also been active as a radio broadcaster. He lives in Hyde Park, on Chicago's South Side, where he was born in 1959.